CW01011065

The Secrets of SUCCESSFUL SPEAKING AND BUSINESS PRESENTATIONS

About the author

Gordon Bell is a lapsed scientist who took refuge in the entertainment business – writing and appearing in films, TV and the theatre. In 1956 he founded Gordon Bell and Partners, a successful organization teaching communications skills for industry and commerce. The company operates not only in the UK but also in many other parts of the world. Gordon Bell practises what he preaches and is in great demand as an experienced speaker. His students range from the heads of large multinational organizations to people at all levels who need to know about speaking.

Books in the series

The Secrets of Successful Business Letters
Clive Goodworth

The Secrets of Successful Copywriting Patrick Quinn

The Secrets of Successful Direct Response Marketing
Frank Jefkins

The Secrets of Successful Hiring and Firing
Clive Goodworth

The Secrets of Successful Leadership and People Management Clive Goodworth

The Secrets of Successful Low-budget Advertising Patrick Quinn

The Secrets of Successful Low-budget Exhibitions
John Powell and Patrick Quinn

The Secrets of Successful Selling Tony Adams

The Secrets of Successful Speaking and Business Presentations Gordon Bell

The Secrets of Successful Telephone Selling
Chris de Winter

The Secrets of

SUCCESSFUL SPEAKING AND BUSINESS PRESENTATIONS

Gordon Bell

Butterworth-Heinemann Ltd
Linacre House, Jordan Hill, Oxford OX2 8DP

OXFORD LONDON BOSTON
MUNICH NEW DELHI SINGAPORE SYDNEY
TOKYO TORONTO WELLINGTON

First published 1987
Reprinted 1988
First published as a paperback edition 1989
Reprinted 1991

British Library Cataloguing in Publication Data
Bell, Gordon
The secrets of successful speaking and business presentations
1. Public speaking
I. Title
808.5′1 PN4121

ISBN 0 7506 0232 5

Printed and bound in Great Britain by
Billing and Sons Ltd, Worcester

Contents

Acknowledgement

Figures 3, 5, and 13 plus a few short passages of text originally appeared in *The Gower Handbook of Management*, and are included in this book by permission of Gower Publishing Company Limited.

INTER-CITY

1 The right frame of mind

When you picked up this book, you did so in response to a somewhat blunt question: 'Do you talk to yourself?' To put it another way, do people really listen to you when you speak? Do they react as a result and, moreover, do they react in the way you would wish them to react? Are the meetings that you conduct or attend as a member stimulating, business-like and a positive spur to beneficial action? Are they?

Most men and women would agree that personal skills in communications are an asset both to themselves and to their own immediate world. So what is your own immediate world? You might be a managing director who has to speak at dinners, conferences, and company meetings. You might be a woman who runs the local institute; an aspiring manager or manageress who must make a presentation to a board of directors; the master of a masonic lodge; a politician; a preacher; a teacher; the president of a sports club; a lecturer in physics; a favourite uncle of the bride; a sports celebrity who could cash in on his (alas, temporary) fame; the incoming mayor – or just you, you with an urge to share your thoughts and opinions.

All over the world there are millions of people who would like to be able to stand on their feet and speak well in public. You are probably one of them. You might be good at it and wish to be even better. Why not? Above all, you will want to be certain that you do not talk to yourself.

But first: what on earth prevents you from rising to your feet, say next Tuesday, and giving a first class talk? I have asked hundreds of men and women that question. Their replies range from calm optimism to blue funk. Fear ranks highest in the majority, sheer terror at the prospect of being asked to speak. Why?

(A note for women readers: I apologize for using words like 'man', 'his', 'him', throughout. Of course women are included in the thinking behind this book.)

In discussing what makes a first class speaker, people usually come up with a list rather like this:

(a) He has something worth saying.
(b) He has time to prepare.
(c) He has experience.
(d) He has personality.
(e) He has confidence.
(f) He looks impressive.
(g) He has a gift for speaking, and so on.

Ask the same people what makes speaking difficult for them, personally, and they reply:

(a) I've nothing worth saying.
(b) I've no experience.
(c) Audiences scare me, I'm nervous, shy.
(d) I have no time to do it properly.
(e) I have an accent.
(f) I'm not an extrovert, can't give a performance.
(g) I lack confidence.

Then follows a string of similar self-pitying excuses.

May I assume that you have the usual faculties of speech and that you have no exceptional physical or mental deficiency? If so please consider the following proposition:

That the only thing that prevents you from speaking effectively is your own vanity, your conceit, your self-centred worry about yourself.

'But,' cries the would-be manager, 'that's not true! I'm shy. I'm nervous. Why, when I get up to speak I tremble and stutter and sweat with fear. I tell the audience how difficult it is for me to face them and that they must excuse me for being unaccustomed to this sort of thing. I don't know how to stand or what to do with my hands so I stuff them in my pockets or fiddle with my notes. Me, conceited! Me? Nonsense! I'm timid, modest, reserved. I'm an introvert and I lack confidence. How can you call that vanity?'

You probably said that very well, with passionate sincerity and looking me bang in the eye. Good.

Now let us calm down and examine the question. Let us look at this fear, sometimes amounting to panic, that afflicts thoroughly nice, normal people when they are asked to speak and need to be at their best. Where was your focus when you stuttered and sweated? On yourself. 'Introvert' you said as if looking inward at yourself was a virtue, as if the words 'I' and 'me' were not the dullest words in the language.

What is an audience interested in? Themselves – first, foremost and all the time. This is a perfectly natural fact of life. Unless and until what you have to say has something to do with them, they switch off. So why not focus on them from the start? Vanity, conceit, too great concern with 'How am I going to do?' and not enough concern with 'How are they, the audience, going to do?' starts the trouble.

This truth is a hard one to face – yet it applies at both ends of the scale. Vanity causes the glib, arrogant, loud-mouthed, no-nerves-at-all-I-can-talk-at-the-drop-of-a-hat chap to subject his audience to a flood of guff and buggaboo. It also causes the timid to worry about themselves at the expense of their listeners.

If you face this fact now, you can save yourself a lot of trouble. But please do not accept this too easily. It is imperative that you consider it seriously. Ask yourself, was I really thinking more of myself than of them? Face this honestly. On whom was your focus? We'll come back to confidence building later on.

The timid one said 'I'm nervous. Audiences scare me.' But why should they? An audience is simply a group of agreeable people much like yourself. They have their problems – family problems, tax problems, health problems, social and business problems – just like you. They come to hear you speak and they come with an immense amount of goodwill. They want you to succeed as a speaker. Please keep that in your mind. They want you to succeed. What they succeed in getting out of your talk is the measure of your success.

Definition: *A successful speaker is a man who gives his audience a success.* The speaker's success stems from the audience reaction. If his audience reacts in the desired manner, the speaker has been effective. There is no other criterion.

Your job as a speaker is to give others a fair exchange for the time and attention they give you – not to worry about yourself. So get your mind firmly on your audience. Once you have accepted an invitation to talk, stop worrying about it and work at it – for their sakes as well as your own. With few exceptions there is no such thing as an audience you need to fear. Just get your focus right and build your success on their goodwill.

Now let us turn the penny over. You must remember that an audience is not in the least bit interested in you or your subject until what you have to say has something to do with them. So obviously you must link what you have to say to them, their needs and their interests.

As long as you know your subject, effective speaking stems almost entirely from a study and consideration of other people. If you did not know what you were talking about you would, of course, have the decency to keep quiet.

Newton's third law of motion says, roughly, 'To every action there is an equal and opposite reaction.' A given stimulus creates the same response if conditions remain constant. Herein lies one of the most important points that a speaker must consider. An audience is never a constant factor. There is no such thing as a production line human being. Everyone is unique. People in an audience vary in social levels, technical knowledge, prejudices, age, sex. Even the same people gathered together at different times or under different conditions can change as an audience.

Effective speaking is a human relationship, not something that one person does alone and in isolation. A speaker wishing to get the desired reaction must obviously begin with a study of the source of the reaction, his listeners. Unfortunately, many speakers begin with themselves and end in disaster.

So, the first point that a would-be speaker must think about is his attitude to his audience. His thinking must be positive and outward – not so much 'What subject am I going to talk about?' as 'How can I create a powerful relationship with my audience using the subject as both the generator and the cement which binds the relationship?' Can you imagine anyone erecting Tower Bridge or building a motorway who would begin by laying the first brick or painting the signposts? A rational man starts with a purpose and a plan. So does a professional speaker – and you, whether you realize it or not, are a professional speaker. If you analyse your job as, for instance, a manager you will find that you do little else but talk and write and discuss. Given equal knowledge of his business, a man who knows how to speak, how to write and when to listen always has the advantage over one who does not.

A new commercial venture goes through many stages before the product is delivered to the customers. Delivery represents only about five per cent of the effort. The original idea has to be conceived, discussed, and thought to make sense. Technical researchers work for months, even years, to bring the idea to such a state that a pilot product emerges. Production machinery has to be bought or built. The marketing people research the probable sales and the customers' needs in relation to the product. Then the launch, the presentation, is calculated, worked on and polished to gain the greatest impact and to achieve the desired reaction.

So it is with speaking. Ninety-five per cent of a first class speech happens before you rise to deliver it. It all seems to be so simple, so natural, so spontaneous. The tremble, the stutter and the sweat must be worked out of your system in the study.

Preparation is all, or nearly all.

2 Preparing an effective talk

Let us look at the basic techniques of preparing a talk – the broad brush approach. Later on we will examine more detailed variations for special occasions such as social talking and talking for business.

Many speakers complain that they have no time to prepare properly. If you know your subject you can prepare a talk in one hour. The method we shall discuss now is the one-hour method. There are three stages, roughly twenty minutes each. (When you have ample time, say, three weeks or six, simply extend each stage accordingly.)

Stage one – Brainstorming

Arm yourself with plenty of large sheets of paper and write down at great speed *every* idea on your subject that enters your mind. Make no attempt to think these ideas through. Get them down in rapid notes, symbols or any other shorthand form that will enable you to recognize them when you arrive at the second stage – the plotting stage. Work rapidly. Work non-stop. Your aim during stage one is quantity and breadth, not depth; to amass hundreds of facts about your subject; various opinions, prejudices, misunderstandings, possible visual aids, thoughts about the audience, the occasion, concrete examples – anything which in any way may bear on your proposed talk. Note direct, oblique, tangential and even remotely relevant facts. Set down page after page of rough notes.

During the first stage it is most important that you concentrate and scribble non-stop at great speed. If time allows, do this several times until you have at least ten times more material than your final talk demands. Fix nothing. Solidify nothing. Bear in mind that what might be old stuff, obvious to you, might well be new or in need of explanation to your listeners. So get it all down. Note everything. *A thought unnoted often disappears for ever.*

Give yourself the advantage of all the options. Review the whole subject. This review jogs your memory, gives you flexibility, acts as a solid background for your talk and can prove particularly helpful if you are required to answer questions. Instead of having to excavate facts from the deep recesses of your mind, you have them near the surface, fresh and ready for use.

Quantity. Now you have raw stuff to work on, stacks of it.

Stage two – The 'P' stage

Purpose

Effective speaking stems, almost entirely, from a study and consideration of other people. First, establish your exact purpose in speaking and get it crystal clear. Is it to inform, to entertain, to persuade? Analyse your purpose – what reaction, what action, do you want from your audience? Write your purpose down, rewrite it, perhaps several times. Make it precise. Get it clear. Know exactly why you are talking. A talk rarely succeeds if the aim, the objective, the reason for it is woolly and undefined.

So get your purpose firmly fixed. Keep it simple and uncomplicated. If you can't write your purpose in a dozen, cogent words, distil it until you can. And have that purpose boldly in front of you from now on, and I mean literally displayed before your eyes all through your preparation. Be thorough about this. Do nothing else until you have got your objective utterly clear.

People

Now that you have a wealth of subject matter and a vividly clear purpose, you must ponder on the real material for your talk – the people who will listen to you. Examine every link they have or might have with your subject, because they will be completely uninterested until what you say has something to do with them. Obvious isn't it? What is their technical level, their social, financial level; what are their needs in connection with you and your subject? Study the people until you can see their view of your subject. You can only put your view across in relation to theirs. If you do not know anything about your audience, you would be well advised to find out at once. A discussion with the organizers, even a telephone call, can prove useful. Get to know your audience and integrate them into your presentation *now*; it will be too late when you are on your feet talking.

So, purpose and people. These two essential elements for an effective talk rarely receive enough thought or attention.

Stop here, please.

You must go no further until you have checked that you have the driving force of a clear purpose working for you. You must go no further until you have developed a real interest in your audience and their needs. These two factors should already be allies helping you to establish a partnership with your audience.

Proposition

Now that you have established exactly what reaction you want, you have other people firmly in your mind as essential partners in your success, you must find a theme, a central idea, a thread to which they (and you) can cling.

Keep this theme running throughout your presentation. So get yourself a theme.

After your talk, what message will your listeners carry away with them? What hard facts supported your thesis? Do not flatter yourself that your audience will remember everything that you said. Decide at this stage in your preparation what basic theme you insist they should remember. As with your purpose, write down your theme and work on it until it becomes simple, straightforward, crystal clear and a stimulus for thought or action.

For instance, what do we remember about Martin Luther King's marvellous speeches? We remember: 'I have a dream'. This motif formed the thread that sticks in the mind. Churchill: 'We shall fight on the beaches . . .' 'Give us the tools and we'll finish the job.' Mark Antony: 'For Brutus is an honourable man.'

If you have Shakespeare's works handy, analyse how with constant repetition Mark Antony manipulates a mob which had been screeching with joy at Caesar's death into action quite the reverse.

Study Henry V's Agincourt speech. 'Once more unto the breach, dear friends, once more, or close the wall up with our English dead' (his listeners – what a proposition) and the glorious battle cry climaxing his speech which persuaded them to a man to fight like tigers to win the day.

Jesus Christ gave us many examples of powerful speaking based on a theme. Here is one: 'It is easier for a camel to pass through the eye of a needle than for a rich man to enter into the Kingdom of Heaven.'

You can probably think of many more. Follow the example of the great speakers. Get yourself a theme: and make it ring. You'll find it works, from the inspirational level to the commercial and social.

Power points

As a roof without support will fall flat, so will a thesis

without facts. When you are sure that you have the first three P's – purpose, people, and the proposition – quite clear, you must concentrate on the fourth, the power points; the hard facts which give strength and truth to your assertions.

Probably you have dozens of facts which maintain your argument. You must not be tempted to trot them all out like a laundry list. A good advocate picks out the one, two or three most powerful convincers and builds his case on them. If, for instance, the man you are defending in court has a cast-iron alibi – he could not have been at the scene of the crime because Her Majesty the Queen was presenting him with an OBE at the time – there is no need to go on about how kind he is to his mother or his generosity to the Lifeboat Fund.

You must separate fact – demonstrable, provable fact – from opinion or assertion: and you must check your facts. Select from your mass of facts the one, two or three most powerful of these facts that support your message. These hard facts form your power points, the big guns, the persuaders. If you do not pinpoint them clearly now, they will not stand out prominently enough in your delivered talk. Limit yourself to a maximum of three major truths at this time. The lesser facts you can weave in later, if necessary, or you can reserve them as supplementaries during question time. We are after a clear, straightforward shape for your talk. Avoid clutter. Now you begin to see a structure. You have a purpose in your mind. You have other people in your mind, you have a clear proposition in your mind and strong facts to support what you say.

Profit

Profit? Do we mean money, increased knowledge, laughter – a feeling of well being? Of course you are not thinking of profit to yourself. You are making sure that your listeners get a profit in exchange for their time. They will be that much older after your talk and they cannot recover lapsed time – it's a bit of their life gone. Please check, quite seriously, that you can see a profit for them from your talk. You will get your own reward in due course. If they have a success so do you.

The P stage, the professional at work:

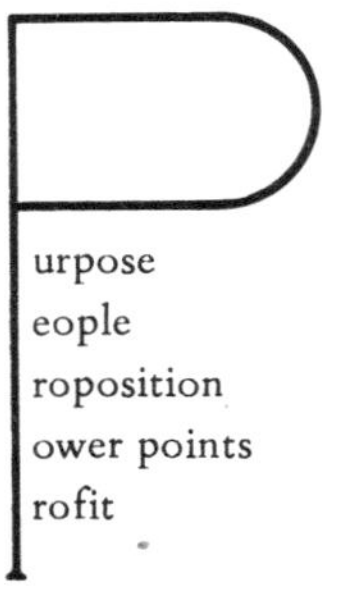

Now let us clear the decks. On the basis of the P stage, arrange your main headings and subheadings into an outline. At first this outline may occupy several pages. Boil it down from several to two or three: then one page only so that you can see the main structure of your talk in a simple form.

That concludes the second stage. Many ideas will have occurred to you while you worked on stages one and two. You will have noted them. They might come in handy at the third stage, which follows.

But before you go on to stage three, stop for a moment and make sure that you have, so far, got your talk under control. Here are a few reminders:

A successful speaker knows his subject and is enthusiastic about it. (If he isn't who else is going to bother? If he hasn't got a fire in his belly how can he set other people alight?)

He makes certain that he is well prepared.

He has considered his audience and believes that the subject is important to them.

Bad speakers are usually people who think about themselves too much. They worry about speaking instead of working at it. The essential questions that must be answered at the end of the second stage are:

(a) What precisely is my subject? The scope of my talk?

(b) Why am I speaking about it to this group of people and what do I know about them?
(c) Have I picked out the main points which must be highlighted? Have I checked the facts which support them?
(d) Have I arranged these power points so that this particular audience will fully understand them and be involved in them?
(e) Have I made sure that there is a glowing dominant theme? (Read it again. Check.)
(f) What will the audience gain from this talk?

Take the trouble to answer these questions at this juncture. You will find that the time invested will pay dividends.

Stage three

Preparing the launch, which, you will remember, must be calculated, worked on and polished to gain the greatest impact and to achieve the desired reaction.

The most important minute in a ten-minute talk is minute eleven. What are they thinking, what action is in their minds, what effect have you created by the time you stop talking? What is the afterglow, the reaction? They will applaud if it is that sort of occasion; but what will they take away with them? Did you get the order, the votes, the budget? Is the knowledge you meant to impart firmly lodged? Are they delighted that they asked you to speak?

It might seem a little perverse, but let us begin this third stage with the impact at the end of your talk. Most good playwrights start with the curtain-line and build up the action to bring the curtain down with the greatest effect. The older type of orator used to call this winding up to a finish the peroration. We'll try to avoid long words like that if we can. We'll call it the climax. This is no time to dither and wander. Cut the waffle. Discipline yourself to make the climax brief and bold. As soon as you have rammed home the summary of the facts supporting your theme (of course, including the audience and their interests), stop talking except for your curtain line, the high, shining crown of your talk. Your last sentence must pack a solid punch. So get it right. Work on it. Try at least six ways of ending – there is nearly always a better one than the one you first thought of. If you will forgive a small joke – make a strong, hard, sharp point and sit down on it.

When you have your impact at the ending thoroughly worked out, it would not be unhealthy for you to have in your mind's eye pictures of people applauding, reaching for their cheque books, offering you thanks and congratulations or whatever else you planned as the effect of your speech. By all means savour the moment: but there are steps to build before you reach the pinnacle. For instance the first step, your opening gambit. Let me give you an example of a truly memorable opening.

The location is Geneva: the occasion an international symposium on such topics as monetary systems, civil administration, effluent control, emergent nations, taxation, cost accountancy, organization of labour, scientific exchange and other such grey matters.

The symposium seemed to have been deliberately designed to be a failure. It was mid-summer with a temperature in the eighties. The air conditioning wasn't working and about twelve hundred heavy breathers with the aromas of all nations added to the fug. Members of the audience wore massive headphones, each ear plus two strands of wire supporting a weight equal to a hardback copy of *War and Peace*. This was the first time I had ever experienced simultaneous translation. The boxes in front of us bore the inscriptions English: French: Spanish: Hindi: German etc. So, if a delegate was speaking in Dutch, one pushed the button for English – only to be greeted by a flood of Spanish. It was that sort of conference.

The programme went thus: morning session, two presentations with a cup of coffee in the interval between them. Afternoon ditto. Evening, after dinner, one presentation and discussion lasting about three hours. And this went on for fifteen solid days, Saturdays and Sundays included, without a break.

The speakers were all eminent authorities, professors of this and that, all high-domed and very important people.

The stage was huge and as each item was announced a grey-head would emerge from the wings carrying under his arm what appeared to be his life's work. He would make his way to the lectern, drop his load on it, switch on the lectern light and proceed to read.

For an hour and a quarter he regurgitated his acquired wisdom and all we had to look at was his bald spot. After what seemed an eternity he would glance up, give us a wrinkled smile and march off with his manuscripts. That was the standard, five times a day for fifteen days!

You can imagine the state of the delegates after ten days. One saw them ground into the carpet with boredom. They looked at their programmes. Next item: The Emergent Nations. Oh God not another one of those! Many people imagine that this subject is new and revolutionary. It was old hat even then. The audience were at prayer, saying to their Maker 'Oh God it's Wednesday. Make it Friday soon. I want to go home. I've had enough of this.' Pity the next speaker. How on earth could anyone bring this lot of zombies to life? They sank deep into their seats as if settling in for hibernation.

Then the finest figure of a man that I'd ever seen walked onto the stage. He was six feet two tall and had shoulders as wide as a doorway. His handsome face was jet black, wet black and shining like a guardsman's boot. He carried not a note and simply came to the centre of the stage and looked at the audience. He did not move. But the audience did. 'Look', they thought, 'look, he's doing nothing. Isn't that interesting?' They sat up. They wriggled towards the edges of their seats and responded to his obvious ease and authority. When he had them completely under control he said, without preamble:

'My mother-in-law does not like me; because my father (pause) ate (pause) her father.'

There followed a shocked silence. Wasn't this a serious conference, worthy and scientific? How dare he!

Then somebody laughed. Then they all laughed. What a relief after so much dry solemnity. They roared and slapped their thighs.

The colossal gentleman did not move. He was a great technician as a speaker. When the laughter had completely subsided – absolute silence, you could hear a feather drop – he continued:

'You laughed just now when I said my father ate another man. But it is true. He did.'

A pause.

'You are all Greeks, French, Americans, British, Chinese, Australasians, Jews, Hindus, Muslims, Christians. You come from all over the earth. You have in your countries centuries of civilization and culture behind you. Yet, if you will forgive me, you are still making economic and political mistakes. My country – one generation removed from cannibalism. Is it surprising that we make mistakes and that we need – oh, ladies and gentlemen, we need – your help.'

What a beginning! He went on to show why and how they could help. And they did. That speech truly moved them to action. Nowhere, nowadays, could this opening be true. Times have changed, thank God. But we must stop there. We are only looking at the possibilities of your getting an impact at the opening of your talk.

Opening gambits

You never get a second chance to make a first impression.

So how will you launch your talk? How will you start? Like sex, effective communication is an intimate relationship with other folk, not something that one does alone. A good speaker is never lonely: he always has his audience taking part, not vocally perhaps but in every other way. Your first duty is to stimulate this state of affairs – the 'us' not the separated you and me. The audience must immediately be made confident that the speaker knows what he is doing. They must find his very first thoughts intensely interesting. This, of course, rules out the usual dreary openings, where, for instance, the speaker talks about himself and his worries as a speaker. Jet-propel yourself off the launchpad and make sure that you firmly strap in your audience and take them with you.

There are functions where it is necessary to observe a set formula such as: 'Your Royal Highness, Mr President, my lords, ladies and gentlemen . . .' If you do not know the form for this particular occasion find out in advance. Toastmasters are delightful chaps with vast experience. In an emergency they will always help if you are so unwise as not to have sorted this out beforehand. If you have been wickedly neglectful and couldn't even get to the toast-master, listen to the preliminaries as he announces you and follow his lead.

For most of us, our speaking is more workaday and not subject to such rarefied atmosphere: but whether you are speaking in white tie and tails or to a group of apprentices in overalls your opening must be skilfully engineered to make the appropriate impact.

You will find the three-sentence technique useful.

Sentence one – you make any vivid, unexpected, offbeat, truly interesting remark you like, always of course bearing in mind your audience.

Sentence two – you link, skilfully, sentence one to your subject and make clear exactly what your subject is.

Sentence three – you *involve* the audience in both your opening remarks and your subject.

Note the technique being used by our friend at the Geneva symposium.

It is essential that you economize and discipline yourself to use only three sentences for this effect. There must be no woolly edges around these three sentences, no 'hums' and 'hahs', no interpolated oddments, no clutter. You are seeking a clean, crisp, immediate communion, a direct response. Experiment until you have got a really good beginning. Excite, link, involve. Do not be satisfied with the first openings you think of: as with your climax, try at least six ways before you decide.

Avoid the word 'I' for at least one minute. Substitute 'you', 'your', or group words describing the audience such as engineers, Scotsmen, managers. Be as specific as you can. Talk about them and their links with the subject. Get the focus firmly on to them and away from yourself.

Pointing the way

As soon as your impact has been achieved and the audience knows what your broad subject is, define your limits so that they will not waste their attention on parts of the subject outside the scope of your talk. Tell them where you intend to take them within your subject, sometimes even which aspects you intend to leave out. From the start concentrate their mental energy on the relevant aspects. Give them clear signposts, briefly.

Signposting establishes several valuable factors. In the first place, it shows that you know where you are going and that there is a logical progression in your talk. Secondly, it defines the limits within which you will work. Supposing for instance that your subject is announced as Nuclear Energy. The very words of the title start a dozen different trains of thought in as many minds. (See Figure 1.)

If you are going to tell them how, in twenty years time, they will be controlling this mad beast at the touch of a switch in their own homes and in their vehicles on the road,

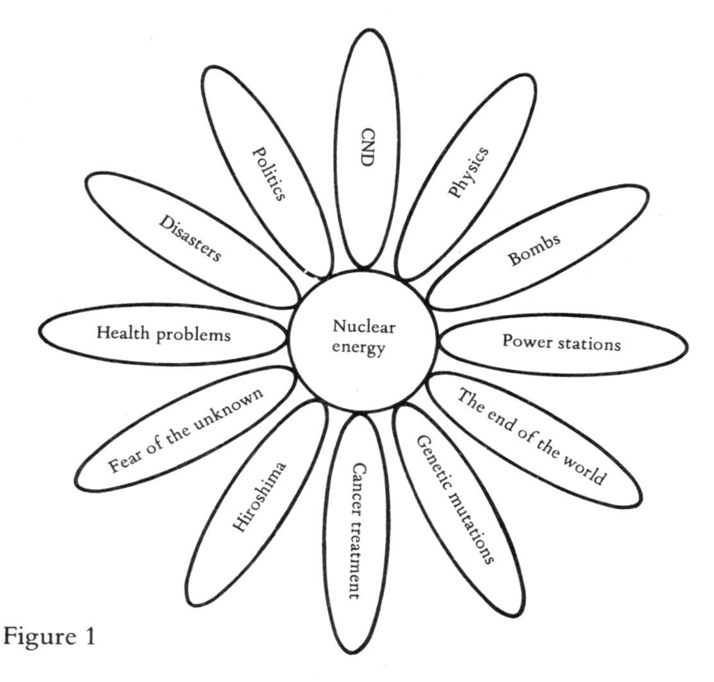

Figure 1

make it clear that these are your limits. Otherwise they will be thinking about children skinned alive or the Cold War or whatever else it is that dominates their thinking about the subject. Confine them within the scope of your talk as early as possible. Take them into your confidence, as it were. Provide them with main footholds. You are already sharing something with them. Watch a racing swimmer as he dives into the water (your impact at opening). The swimmer does not immediately strike out – he settles before his first muscular strokes (signposting period while you gather yourself for your exposition).

Now, you have a dynamic purpose in your mind; you and your audience know where you are going. They have been intrigued by your opening remarks and are ready for the statement of your basic theme, ready for the development of your first power point supporting that theme – and they are eager to find out how and where they fit in with what you have to say.

The elements are prepared for you – the catalyst – to do your work. Several steps are now solidly built – your opening; pointing the way; your theme and the main facts in support; the ending.

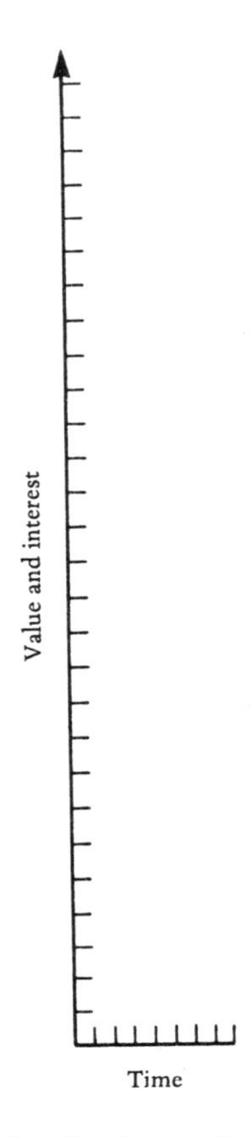

Figure 2 *Axes for graph of value and interest against time. Use the proportions shown here to prepare the graph described in the text.*

To complete the structure, let us have a look at it in another form. Please arm yourself with a pencil and a sheet of paper because we are going to create a graph. Draw the axes exactly as they are in Figure 2. I would appreciate your comments on it and your physical co-operation. To begin with, here are the axes. Draw the axes exactly. Then proceed to Figure 3. Yes, the axes are disproportionate – but please keep these odd ratios in your mind. Let the horizontal axis represent time. Let the vertical axis represent the value and interest you bring to your listeners in that time. You should never take more of your audience's time than is necessary to do your speaking job properly. The value and interest line should be as high as possible in the time they give to you.

Now, please fill in the graph for your own planned talk, as shown in Figure 3.

The shading at the foot of Figure 3 represents the grey sludge area at the beginning of so many talks, during what the poor speaker calls 'warming up'. The monologue here tells how unaccustomed the speaker is and what a trying ordeal he is experiencing in facing such a difficult, awesome set of people. In general, the self-centred blockhead isolates himself and destroys the goodwill of the audience by focusing in the wrong direction. No wonder he is nervous. No wonder the audience already begin to doubt whether they should have come.

Eliminate the sludge area altogether. Instead, get some vigour, elevation and impact into your beginning. Hoist the value-and-interest line clean through the sludge up to X, which marks your impact at opening.

Signposts help your listeners to concentrate on the special aspects of the subject that you intend to cover. Define your limits, briefly.

Now drive towards your first main point (a). You have it clear. You have already worked out how to make your facts come to life, how to link your vivid examples both to the

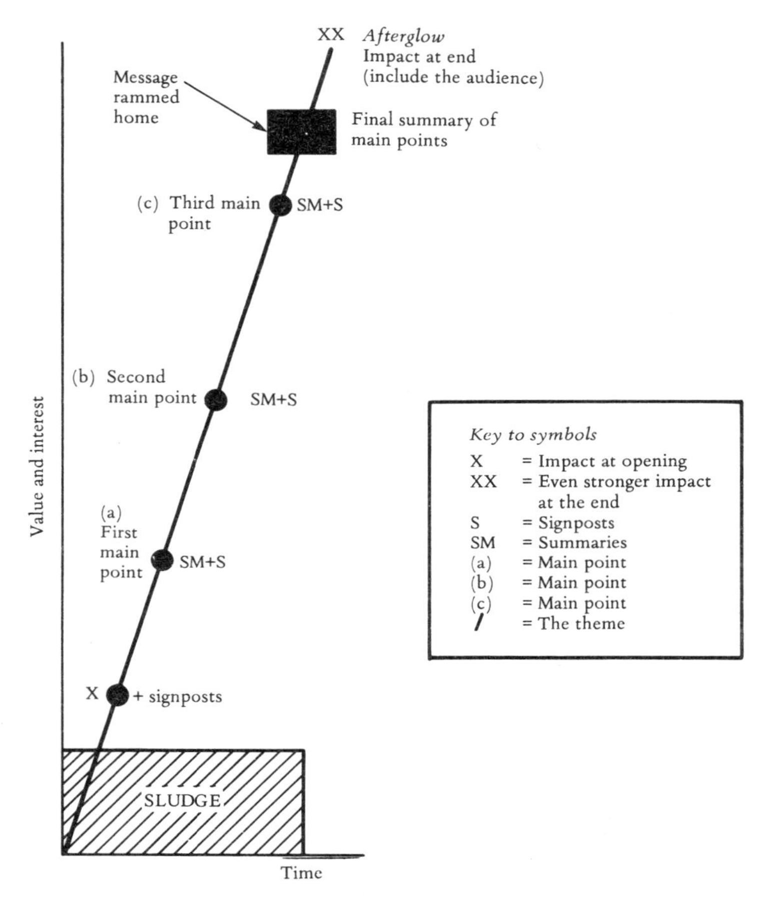

Figure 3 *Graph of value and interest against time.*

facts and to your audiénce. Follow your line, the theme, and support that theme with facts. Develop your message.

Summaries are a matter for your judgement. At least you must make certain that each main point holds fast in the minds of your audience before you tackle the next point.

Signposting internal to the talk, again, is a matter for you to decide. Will summaries and signposting help your audience? If so, use them.

When you reach the climax of your talk, when you ram home your message you must remind your audience of the main facts which support your theme. Summarize crisply: remind them how the matter of your talk affects them and do have a powerful line at the end.

Now that you have your skeleton, give it a body, give it life, warm flowing blood and a personality.

The word personality cannot easily be defined. It is not merely a combination of looks, intelligence, idiosyncrasies and so on. There is much more to it – most of which baffles precise definition. But we can measure it. How do other people respond to what is called one's personality? Responses vary enormously – one man's favourite is someone else's poison. Nobody pleases everyone – in fact it is said that if someone, somewhere, doesn't hate your guts you haven't got any personality at all. Responses measure you as a person, as a speaker, as a communicator. Communication. There's another word that gets bandied about. What does that one mean? It stems from the Latin verb *communicare* which means to share. From it we get words like communism, community, commune, commonwealth, communion (we go to church and share in a sacrament) and common. Your listeners should share what you have; they should, as a result of your talk, have thoughts and opinions in common with you.

A professor in America was rabbiting on about something being a one-way communication. When his students had gone, I said:

'Jack, you're talking nonsense' (we are old friends). 'If it is one-way it is not a communication.'

Talking may be one-way, and often is. Communication starts only when other minds understand and process the data and then complete the cycle by responding. (See Figure 4.)

Throughout your entire speech you must keep your

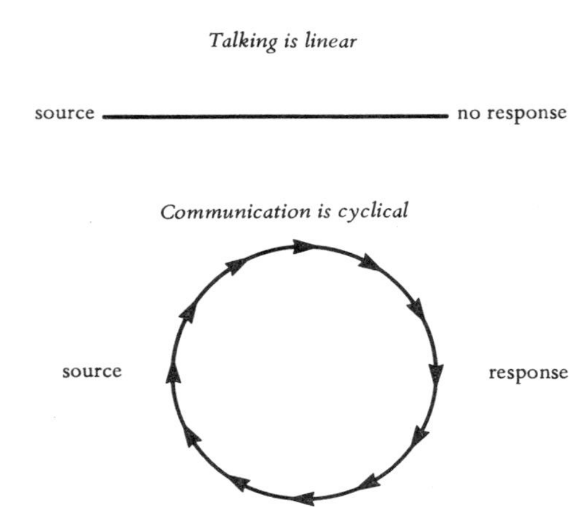

Figure 4

audience in cyclical contact with you and, at least mentally, taking part – sharing your mind. A communicator stimulates response and builds up to added responses point by point.

First class speakers plan to communicate with a purpose not merely to vocalize.

3 Delivering the goods

You will realize that more work has to be done before your talk is ready; but perhaps the best way for us to think this through together is for you to make a start. Let us get you on to the platform and have a rehearsal. Your preliminary reconnaissance now begins to pay off. You will have, if feasible, got to know the hall, the room, the theatre, and noted possible visuals and examples from its size, shape, decorations – that chandelier might be useful – and other features. After all you and the audience have already one thing in common, the location. Even if someone else has been responsible for the stage management – tactfully check everything. Go into the auditorium and check sight lines for visuals. Check the acoustics, check your props – see that they are in working order. Try out microphones if you are using them. Check your films, slides, projector and all other equipment. Above all get to know the local man who works in the place. It is his hall. You can make him an asset and a partner in your success or a flaming nuisance.

Assuming that you will have a chairman to introduce you, have a word with him, too. Whatever you do, don't tell him all about your talk. Many a chatty chairman has spilt the beans and pre-empted most of the speaker's main points. Give him enough to introduce you, no more: name, rank and number as it were. Also, arrange to get him off the platform, if the situation allows, otherwise he'll sit there with egg on his face all through your talk and distract the audience. Unless he is likely to babble on and ruin what you have built up, he might be permitted to come back at question time or to thank you and to bring the proceedings to a close.

Of course, a competent chairman will not want to be seen twiddling his thumbs. He knows that his job is to build up the main attraction – briefly, please sir, briefly – and then adroitly to efface himself. If he can get you a round of applause as you rise, so much the better. A star actor works with more zest if he gets a reception on his entrance: and so will you.

By arrangement with you, the chairman will either tell the audience that questions will follow the presentation or leave it to you to include that news early in your talk. Whether you handle question time solo or the chairman returns to make it more formal should also be decided beforehand. If you have a skilful chairman treasure him, bless him and thank your lucky stars.

Right. Here we go. In one minute you will be on. You say that you are tense, that the adrenalin is racing. Good. You should be keyed up. In fact, if you are not tense – beware! You should be before you start. The most experienced speakers know this feeling and they also know its value. That tension forms part of the dynamic force which will soon be working between you and your listeners. You won't be keeping it to yourself much longer. If you are seated, in view, while somebody introduces you, see to it that your lungs are filled. Deep breathing is a wonderful relaxer and it ensures that your first words have resonance and power. An old trick is to have something amusing running through your mind – any bit of nonsense will do – goosey goosey gander – anything that will bring a faint smile to your face and stop you looking grim.

Now you are on your feet and move towards the position you have decided on for the opening. Every sportsman will know the value of getting feet right. Ask a golfer, or a tennis player making a backhand drive. Your stance should not be rigid but it must be right. Stand on both feet with your body upright and well balanced. You haven't any visible notes. An actor who appears reading from his script, or Tosca bringing on the score with her, would soon lose the audience's confidence. Obvious notes are signs of ill-completed preparation. If your theme and main points are so complicated that even you, the expert, need a sheaf of notes to follow it, how can you expect the audience to keep track? Clarify, simplify. Notes belong to the study. They form a barrier between you and your listeners. Learn to do without them while you are speaking. At the very least, reduce them to a bare minimum, say ten key words boldly printed in heavy letters about one and a half inches high, so that you can read them rapidly from any part of your working area – should you really need them. If you wish to quote a list of precise figures or someone else's words, simply pick up a note and read it. That is fair enough. But your own material should be so well groomed that it seems spontaneous. Try to make at least your first major point without recourse to notes. Don't lose your audience's eyes by reading. You have an advantage over play actors. They are rarely able to look an audience straight in the eye and address them directly. You can and you must look them in their collective eye and address them directly. Let them see your mind at work through your eyes.

Start the cyclical effect. From now on, you will be studying their minds, watching and genuinely interested in their early reactions. If you are clearly interested in them, they will return the compliment. Work with them not at them. You are no longer on your own. You have company – eager to share what you offer. Nerves! What are they? By now you are so busy concentrating on your audience you've forgotten about yourself. Now get on with giving them some value.

You will find this first, rough-cut rehearsal more productive if you go straight through from beginning to end without interruption. If you have a few colleagues helping you, invite at least one plain, blunt fellow who will be critical. Fulsome backscratchers do more harm than good. Insist on criticism. If you feel, on consideration, that the critic is mistaken you can disregard him; but he may be right and lead you to correct some fault. After all, you'll get the credit for this. You don't have to put in the programme 'additional dialogue by so and so'. Pick his brain. Use him. Don't put up defences. Listen.

Go straight through, please. This run will enable us to get an idea of the time taken by your talk, to see the whole shape and how it is built. Let's try it out, shall we? There will probably be a few suggestions afterwards. Start the stopwatch! Please begin.

★ ★ ★

The Talk

★ ★ ★

Stop the watch! Good. You took a little under the time allowed. You can use that spare time when you are actually working with an audience, weighing responses and developing their thoughts, at their pace. Allow about twenty per cent extra for the real presentation. You'll need it.

Your structure was excellent – a good idea to open with; signposts clear and brief, tactful summaries. I liked that notion of yours to link one of your internal summaries to St Paul's well known example. 'So there are these three things, faith, hope and charity – and the greatest of these is charity.' Your three points were more earthy but the parallel made them stick in the mind. Your final summary had the force of brevity, fact and clarity; and your build-up to the climax carried a power that reflects the work you must have done on it. Splendid.

To go back to your opening remarks or rather to the moments just before them. You will recall that effective speaking is a human relationship and it is the speaker who has to create the atmosphere within which that relationship can flourish – even before he says a word. Don't rush your fences. Take your time. A smile does not mean a nervous grin or a baring of the teeth. A real smile starts in your innards – when you feel good all over and it comes out in your face. Let it happen because you truly feel genial towards your audience. Take a look at them with geniality in your mind and they will respond by being genial.

When you switch on the radio and the tuning is not right or the volume too low, you can make adjustments to suit yourself. Members of an audience cannot do this except for the few who can furtively turn up the volume on their hearing aids (or switch them off!). You've got to help everyone to tune in to you, the young ones with no problems; others with accumulations of wax and the downright hard of hearing. You might have to cope with latecomers, the shufflers, the coughers, the gossips, et al. Of course you make no attempt to talk above the clatter. If you accept such a show of bad manners at the start you run the risk of that being the standard. So without being pompous or tetchy about it get them under control and prepared for your opening remarks.

Tune them in. This might mean that you have to raise your volume a little and even be somewhat deliberate in delivering your first few ideas. Your opening is so good; you will want them to receive its full value.

Now, how are they doing? You have opened well, your audience is at ease and confident. They know that the subject concerns them. The lively interesting manner in which you presented your first few thoughts has stimulated them to want more. You have planned to give them more. Stick to your theme, stick to your main points. Keep your original purpose firmly in mind and work to achieve it – through them. Never leave them out of anything you do or say. On this last point you have room for improvement. Some of your facts seem downright dull and remote from this particular audience. There are no dull subjects. Everything under the sun teems with interest. From even such beginnings as a dirty ashtray or the Industrial Training Act a lively mind could create a fascinating talk. How are you going to tell your story, to give your facts their full value as facts plus that life which also gives them interest? The key to power in story-telling is to bind everything you say to people and things – the concrete rather than the abstract. You might well be talking about some entirely abstract technical concept. Human beings and physical, tangible things judiciously woven into your presentation will vitalize even the unlikeliest subject for a potent talk. Also, whenever you can, link your examples directly to your listeners. It's their talk; use their experience in examples. An earthquake killing thousands in China could leave your audience unmoved: but a gas explosion in Clay Street, Manchester, will engender great interest – especially to those of your audience who live in Clay Street, Manchester.

Facts are sacred and must not be tampered with. Concrete examples emphasize facts and make facts stick in the mind. The closer the examples are to the experience and the environment of the audience the more surely your points will find their target. Contrary to a common opinion, facts do not always speak for themselves. They need good men to speak for them. No fact of life need be colourless or less interesting than fiction. You must skilfully develop the story of each fact – yes, the story – giving it a good beginning, a lively motif, substance, excitement, and strong close-to-home examples. Work out three audience-orientated examples for each of your main facts and use the best of them.

You maintained good eye contact with us except when you introduced visual aids.

Voice

Please study Figure 5. Which effect do you consider the more stimulating, line A or line B?

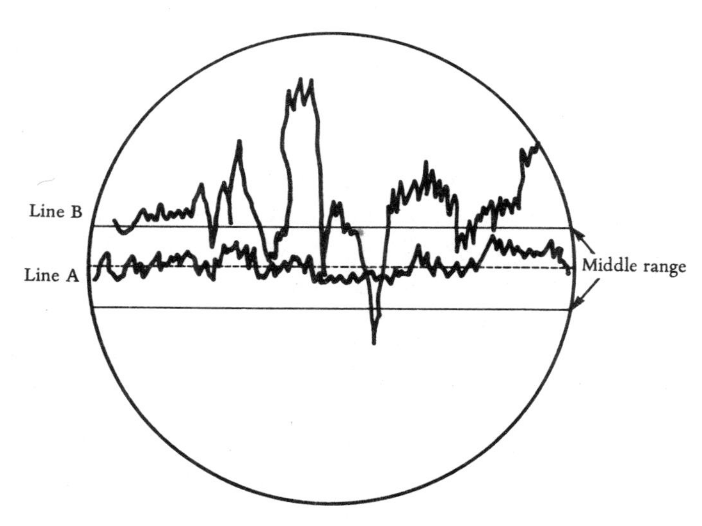

Figure 5

You probably found line A flat and dreary; line B, with its peaks and troughs and vigorous variations, much more interesting. Your voice loitered around A almost throughout your talk. It is reasonable that most of your talk should be encompassed by the middle range but do break out occasionally. Let your voice reflect your enthusiasm and your urgent wish to make your points. What is significant must be made so. Ring a few vocal changes. Vary the pace of your voice, vary the pitch. Pauses can have a great effect.

Use silence. Don't be afraid to stop to allow the ideas to sink in. If you can command attention during a silence, use silence, but sparingly and under control.

A hypnotist wishing to put someone to sleep employs a subdued, monotonous voice and a single soporific thought repeated and repeated until the patient gives up and slumbers. To arouse the patient he makes some sharp noise and brings his own voice to life by using a complete change of tone. The patient wakes up.

Many people fuss and fret about their voices. If you mumble incoherently or bellow like a sergeant major you are simply being rude and inconsiderate. Use enough voice to ensure that everybody hears – comfortably – what you are saying. People cannot apply their full mental energy to your thoughts if they use most of it just to hear your words.

Human voices possess an immense range of volume, tone, pace, attack. Why be monotonous? Why be dull? Why mutter or bawl? Why not work out beforehand how you can give variety and appropriate vocal values to each part of your talk? Think in terms of main headlines and paragraphs and make sure that each new idea comes to the audience with a change in vocal approach. Particularly when introducing a fresh point, give your voice a lift. Watch sentence length; see to it that a few crisp short ones intervene between a series of protracted sentences. Watch the ends of the sentences. Lift them. A rising pitch holds more interest than a dying fall.

'But', you say, 'what about my accent? I have an accent.' So what? Who hasn't? If you have Bradford in your voice – good, you come from Bradford. It's the truth, isn't it? What is wrong with that? You have got to present the best that is truly you, not a phoney imitation of some wry-necked duke. Be yourself – at your best. Accent is not the same as dialect, however. Most Cockneys will understand 'I was goin' up the apples and I bumped me uncle'. This, translated, means I was going up the (apples and pears) stairs and I bumped my (Uncle Ned) head. Simple rhyming slang – simple for Londoners but incomprehensible elsewhere. Please do not use dialect unless you are speaking to people who will appreciate it. But if you normally say 'brass' not 'brahss', say 'brass'.

Distractions

Has anybody ever told you that you pepper your talk with phrases like 'in fact', 'as a matter of fact', even 'as a matter of actual fact'? I lost count after the first dozen or so and also lost track of your thoughts while bothering about it. You know that 'in fact' should only be used as an opposite to 'in theory'; otherwise often repeated mindlessly, it becomes a distracting mannerism. You must get rid of it. Fortunately you are free from the oddities that afflict many speakers – sometimes to the annoyance of the audience, sometimes to their ill-concealed glee. For instance, a colleague called me into his conference room where he was conducting a speaking workshop and asked me to hear one of the participants. I don't remember a word the man said, only that throughout his talk he had his right arm over the top of his head and he was excavating his left ear with his right forefinger. He was astonished when it was pointed out to him.

On another occasion a computer man entertained us while giving a presentation on time sharing. We never discovered – at least from this chap – what time sharing was about but he triggered much joy and many a smothered giggle. His talk illustrated perfectly the danger of misusing an overhead projecter. Believe it or not, he planted himself between the projector and the screen with the full beam of light focused on his sweatshirt, which bore the legend *Winchester.* He swayed from side to side, in and out of the light, and we read *Win*, *Winch*, *inch*, *chester*, *hester*, *Winchester*, *Win*, again and again. How can anyone be so crass. Sadly, some can.

Most of us have at least one candid friend who will tell us about the distracting things we do or say. Ask your friends to tell you before you get in front of a full audience yearning to do so.

It is a truism that actions speak louder than words. If your body sends out distress signals we lose confidence in your words. We watch you wriggling or estimate how many coins you are jingling in your pockets. We wonder what it is that interests you so much outside as you stride to and fro and gaze out of the window. Why do you stand like a teapot and wave your spout-hand around while the handle-hand remains fixed? Have you no handkerchief? Need you knuckle away dewdrops so often? Must you emphasize every word by poking the air or gesticulating like a windmill learning semaphore? My artist friend (Charles Peattie) has illustrated some of the strange postures that speakers adopt in Figure 6. You will recognize most of them.

People ask 'What can I do with my hands if I can't stuff them in my pockets?' Should your managing director ask you to see him would you walk into his office with your hands thus stowed away? Of course not; it would be thought disrespectful. So to start with it's rude. Secondly, and much more importantly, if you are still worrying about yourself, demon vanity still lurks around. Ask yourself 'What did the good God do with your hands?' He gave you shoulders from which hang upper arms, from which hang forearms and wrists, from which hang hands. Newton again – gravity. Leave them alone in their natural position at your side – until you want to use them to show a direction, indicate a size or shape or to emphasize a point – naturally and without fuss. Above all, deliberately concentrate and regain contact with those people in front of you. You should be so interested in them that 'What can I do with my hands?' is a nonsense. Stop focusing inward. Concentrate on someone else. You'll forget about your hands. Try it. You'll find it works.

The Teapot
Reluctant nudist
The Walker
Must keep my trousers up
The scratcher
The table-crawler
Hair pusher
Hand-washer
When's he going to drop it?

Figure 6

That reheasal has given you some clues about likely reactions. Next please read the chapter on visual aids (see page 103) and weave in the ideas contained in it. Then use the checklist as an aide-mémoire to revise and to strengthen your talk.

Checklist

Structure

Impact at opening:	Is it alive? Does it involve the audience? Does it start an agreeable relationship?
Signposts:	Do they show where you are all going together: outline the scope; give the audience footholds, a plan of the route? Are your indicators clear – and brief?
Theme:	Does the proposition maintain a strong line throughout the talk?
Main points:	Are the facts supporting your proposition authoritative, justified, and truly significant?
Interim summing up:	Check point – have you driven your facts home so far? Do you need internal signposting to lead them on to the next point?
Final summing up:	The build-up to the climax. Make your main facts unforgettable. Involve the audience. Not too long.
Impact at ending:	Re-state and achieve your objective. Action on their part? Curtain line creating the afterglow. Clean-cut? Alive? Positive?

Presentation

The Story line:	Will they understand your lang-

	uage? Do you create pictures in their minds; include them? Real close-to- home examples. People and concrete things – not woolly abstractions? Are you developing the theme? Does the heart of the matter throb?
Audience contact:	Can they see your mind at work through your eyes? Are you watching and interested in them; building on their reactions?
Visual aids:	Appropriate, simple, clear, memorable?
Voice:	Remember line A and line B. Get variety and be generous.
Mannerisms:	You've eliminated the distractions?
Time:	Are you sufficiently within the time set to allow for more time needed when 'working' the audience?

Exercise

Here is a quick exercise which should provide a little fun for you. Try the one-hour method in miniature. You've got a quarter of an hour.

Select any of these ten words: money, hooligans, zero, holes, dust, fire, horses, prejudice, cookery, fish.

Stage one: five minutes rapid fire brainstorming, noting all the ideas on the subject that come to mind. Five minutes only. Non-stop. Scribble, speed, quantity.

Suppose you choose fire. Stage one might come out something like this:

Early man – discovery advantage over animals. Religion, sun, volcanoes. Insurance, house fire, fire drill, fire at sea. Safety at work or in home. Fire in speech – passion, love.

Bush fire, South of France forest fire (Nice). Crops ruined, people scarred – plastic surgery, heat, motor racing, furnace fire, industry, steel, steam engine, appliances, engines, fire brigade, burns unit, chemical warfare. Ladders, building regulations, Nero, Rome. Poetic fire. Burns, asbestos, spark plugs, gun fire, fireworks, firewater, alcohol, fire boats, fire fighting, camp fire, boy scouts rubbing sticks. Sack – dismissal, ashes. Fire regulations, bonfires, Guy Fawkes – parliament, fire bombs, napalm, atomic fire. Costs – money. Electric fire comfort, cooking, coal, steam, oxygen and fuel plus heat. Smoke. The Pope is chosen. Cigarettes, pipes, social problems, dirt, cremation . . . and so on. The list is limitless but five minutes will do for now. Please pick out your own word and start. Go for quantity.

Stage two: purpose of talk? To whom? To get across what message? Main facts, profit for audience. Five minutes only.

Stage three: fives minutes. Select, decide main line. How start? Development of facts. Examples. Visuals. Summary. How end?

See the whole short talk has a clear shape, purpose and impact. If you can do that in fifteen minutes with a random subject, what might you achieve with more time and something you really know about?

Work this exercise every day for a fortnight instead of doing the crossword. It will do you much more good.

4 Talking for business

As a director, a manager, an aspiring manager you will be interested in facts. A survey of over 5000 men and women such as yourself revealed the following data:

(a) On average, they had received about fourteen years of formal education.
(b) Approximately a third of them gained degrees, diplomas and other paper qualifications.
(c) Only one in twenty-three felt that their subsequent achievements in life matched their abilities.
(d) Fewer than one in twelve had taken the trouble to equip themselves with skills such as effective speaking, clear writing, handling meetings.

From the chairman of the largest industrial group to supervisors and staff, everybody uses words. Every businessman and businesswoman writes letters, reports, memoranda, orders. Reasonable people will agree that words are a vital tool in industry. The higher we go up the ladder of management the more important words become.

Many business meetings produce nothing but frustration and expense. The average executive spends a third of his working life talking at interviews, conferences, committees (to say nothing of the time and hassle involved in arranging them and getting there). How much of this talk is productive? How many businessmen are either confident or competent when making a presentation or delivering a speech?

The nub of effective management is communications. Time and effort that you invest in developing your own skills as a communicator must produce dividends. Speaking is for other people. This fact about effective speaking is so obvious and so simple that many overlook it. An audience always evaluates a speaker subjectively. What did they get from the talk? The answer to this question measures the speaker.

A manager needs to command attention at conferences and other meetings; he must be able to make oral presentations to his board and to professional organizations: to brief his staff, to persuade, to convince. Particularly if he is a specialist, he must be able to clarify specialized concepts so that others, not necessarily qualified, can share his thoughts. Even the most brilliant man is useless until his ideas can be shared by others who can use them.

A successful speaker is a man who gives his audience a success. Many managers, both male and female, suffer from the delusion that speaking in public is the same as a theatrical performance, or something suitable only for extroverts. This delusion often serves as a defence. The plain truth is that they fear exposure of their limitations as speakers. This state of affairs is deplorable. If people have something worth saying, they should not only say it but also learn how to say it with full effect. 'Why should the devil have all the good tunes?' asked General Booth. It is also pertinent to ask, 'Why should the image-makers and the tricksters have a monopoly of effective speech?'

Many businessmen have to recommend changes that will cost money. In most companies there is a procedure for this. The proposer has first to submit a document setting out his proposal in detail. This goes through the normal channels and may sometimes be accepted or rejected as it stands. More frequently the proposer will be asked to appear before a board or committee to explain his proposal or to answer questions about it. The written part of the proposal is a persuasive report and should be conceived with that in mind. The oral presentation is part speech, part meeting and part interview. It is a speech but it must be disguised in delivery so that it does not sound like one.

A successful speaker is a man who gives his audience a success. Nowhere is this concept more important than in a boardroom. Directors are busy men and women. You want something from them. You are not the only one. You must not inflict a hard sell on them. Give them reasons, firmly supported, why they, in accepting your proposition, can feel that they have made a shrewd decision. What you seek is agreement.

Imagine that you have a chap on the floor. You have your foot on his neck and a loaded gun in your hand. Six of your friends, big, burly prop-forward types, all carrying guns, also menace this unfortunate wretch. You stamp on his face, cock your gun and snarl 'Do you agree?' What does he say? He says 'Yes'. Your friends go home. You put your gun away and turn your back on the wretch only to find that there is a knife in it – in your back, I mean. Because what you got was not agreement, it was surrender. Failure to understand the difference between these two words causes most of our industrial troubles. Surrender rarely settles anything for long. Agreement works.

Please etch into your mind this thought about case presentation: the surest way to gain agreement is through self-interest – the other fellow's self-interest.

Your presentation should demonstrate that it is in their interests to agree to do what you ask of them. You have three keys to open their minds. They are: their *need*, their *greed*, and their *self-esteem* (status). Work on whichever is apt or on all three.

The most congenial way to live is to be busy with a product that truly fulfils a human need. Any job without a strong element of service in it gives no satisfaction, except to the twisters and the crooks: and even they, when looking in the mirror must sometimes say 'Ugh!' and reach for the toilet roll.

A first class proposal will solve your listeners' problem. They have a need for what you propose. So there is no requirement for you to be a smart aleck or to con them. Lasting, successful business is about trust and repeat orders. Customers never surrender twice. They go elsewhere.

Circumstances vary. You might be a director talking to your fellow directors, a manager presenting a proposal within the company. You might be a salesman from outside persuading them to give you an order; someone asking a bank for a loan; a builder seeking planning permission or even a cabinet minister trying to squeeze out more for his department. Many of you will be well trained and experienced in these matters. Please bear with me. Perhaps you have colleagues or juniors who represent you less than perfectly. Here is a chance for you, tactfully, to put them in the picture. Give them this book, or lodge it in your company library. I cannot cover every situation, so I'd be grateful if you would adapt what follows to your own conditions.

Decision-makers rarely have time to read long, complicated reports. Instead they ask for an oral presentation. As an additional saving, the board will sometimes arrange for other interested people to attend. Are you going to waste their time? Of course not. You will prepare for them thoroughly, professionally. Recently I saw and heard a man wreck his career by making a hash of things in front of his own top management. His excuse – he hadn't time to prepare. The fact that he spent two hours daily over a boozy lunch did not occur to him as stupid. You can have lunch every day of your life but not a golden opportunity to get influential people sharing your views. 'There is a tide in the affairs of men which taken at the flood, leads on to fortune.' Don't miss the tide. Do your homework.

In preparing a presentation the proposer should ask himself questions which demand answers.

1 Do you know exactly what you want? Exactly? You cast your bread upon the waters. Do you do so just for the pleasure of watching the ducks feed? Or is your real intention to catch a duck for dinner? You will recognize echoes of the P stage. Purpose. People. Proposition. Power points. Profit. Sometimes your purpose may be to get immediate action this day. Sometimes only to build the first steps – perhaps to persuade a potential customer to visit your plant to see the machine you are selling in operation. You might have a main purpose or options leading to it as a compromise. Think your purpose through meticulously. Why are you there? What outcome do you seek?
2 Do you really believe in your case? If you do not, drop it at once, otherwise it might become a millstone round your neck. But of course you do fervently believe that it is a good thing. So we'll proceed.
3 Have you got all the facts that support your case and have you checked them?
4 What are the strongest arguments for your case?
5 What are the benefits to your listeners? The answers to 4 and 5 should be identical. No argument has more power than that those who decide also benefit.
6 Why must the present situation be changed? What is their problem, repeat, *their* problem?
7 Who else is affected (unions, other divisions, etc.)?
8 Is there an alternative to your plan? Can you give them options? At least let them see that you have looked at other ways of solving their problem (but the facts show that your way is best for them).

9 What are the arguments against your plan? Do not attempt to dodge this question. If you are not prepared to demonstrate that your scheme outweighs any conflicting factors, you are vulnerable. So show that the benefits are clearly more important to them than any drawbacks. You ignore alternatives and snags at your peril. If you are not ready to examine them someone on the board may bring them up. That puts him among the opposition and the meeting may end up by discussing his views rather than yours.
10 To what men and women are you presenting your plan? Get to know something about each one. Do you know who your probable allies and opponents are? Should you do any lobbying? Do you need to?
11 Have you discussed the finances with the experts? You must get the money right.
12 Have you prepared handouts of any complicated figures, maps, charts, etc?
13 Have you prepared a really compelling case? (Time plus the value-interest ratio are particularly important in the boardroom.)
14 How will you sum up? Plan it.
15 Will your ending motivate the action you seek? Plan it.
16 Are you ready for questions?
17 Have you firmly emphasized the benefits that they (your listeners) will gain?

Remember: nothing induces agreement quicker than self-interest. For all practical purposes the board only wants to know the answer to one question. Have they a problem and does your proposal solve it for them?

Ask yourself will your proposal satisfy their need, their greed, their self-esteem – or all three?

A few boards of directors run their meetings like a Star Chamber – stiff, formal, no nonsense. In general, directors aim to be business-like and, if a little hilarity creeps in occasionally so much the better. The larger a meeting the more need for formality. But usually a working board will consist of, say, eight to ten people, sometimes more, sometimes fewer, with perhaps a specialist or two called in as advisers. This is the sort of board you are likely to face with a business proposition. They will be relaxed and at ease in their own territory, but if you notice that the production director has whipped off his jacket, lit up a cigarette and planted his feet on the furniture, don't be tempted to emulate him. The chairman will probably ask you to take a seat. Do so. Unless you are known, he will introduce you to the members. Discreetly check each name against the table plan you have prepared. A man's name is the most important sound in the world – to him – so get it right, and use it.

You'll need the chairman on your side so give him your attention. Regard him as your guide through the preliminaries and keep him with you. Don't grovel. Directors despise crawlers – they meet too many of them – but this does not mean that you can be cocky. Later, you are going to take over but bide your time.

You are given the cue to begin. Do you stand or do you sit? If you have the option, stand up to gain command and eye contact with the board members. You will have stage managed your presentation earlier on – perhaps by arrangement with the secretary. Your equipment has been checked, you know where the switches are and everything else you require is to hand. Before you have said a word the board realizes that you intend to be business-like and know what you are doing.

Your impact at opening must not be theatrical or clever-clever. Such tricks are counterproductive in a boardroom and annoy people who want to get on with the job. Whatever you do, do not start with something like 'I want you to give me two million pounds for . . .' Their response is 'Oh, do you?'. Or 'I am going to persuade you (convince you) . . .' 'Oh, are you?'. Their defences begin to rise.

Hardly the birth of a good relationship. But your opening must have impact. What better than profit in the first sentence?

A well tried structure to work with is shaped by these questions:

What?
Why?
How?
Who?
Where?
When?

What? – at a well-run meeting, the agenda indicates what the proposal is about. A good chairman will also have made it clear in introducing the item. Nevertheless you use it in your opening something like this:

Mr Chairman (or his name), ladies and gentlemen, as you know, the proposal is that we install six new Gumbil machines at a cost of £1,000,370 (which will bring you an additional profit of £420,000 each subsequent year within three years of installation). The chairman didn't mention that last bit, but you've already got their ears flapping and money working in their minds. Your theme is benefits, profit. Now what you have to do is to substantiate your assertion.

You are probably the least wealthy, least powerful person in the room, but you've got to be in control during your presentation – in company with the chairman. The yes yes yes technique will help you. When you have delivered your opening, turn to the chairman 'for his guidance'. Ask him 'This proposal will take about six minutes. Will that be all right?'

'Yes', says the chairman. He had feared it would take longer.

'And you'd rather I answered questions after the presentation so as not to interrupt the flow?'

'Yes', says the chairman.

'With your permission, I propose to do it this way – first the problem, then the suggested solution, and finally show a balance sheet and where your profit comes from.'

'OK', says the chairman. 'Yes, that's fine.'

The chairman has given you three 'Yeses' and not only is he being positive. All round the table people are nodding heads and giving affirmative signs – partly to keep in with the boss but mostly because it makes sense and they agree anyway. Agree. That's what you aim to get, agreement. You want to start them 'yesing' and keep them 'yesing' all through, especially to obtain the final 'yes'.

There are dangers that you must cater for. So rehearse your opening and allow for variations. If you get two good 'yeses' and you feel that the third question might bring 'yes, yes – get on with it!' don't risk the third. The chairman might say 'Six minutes. Can't you do it in five?' A negative response which you must turn round. 'So you'd like me to do it in five minutes? Yes.'

Some people almost beg for the negative by shaping the questions for a 'no' answer. e.g. 'You don't want me to take any longer than six minutes, do you?'

'No.'

You need to be brisk, brief and flexible in working for a positive start. When you succeed in stimulating the 'yes, yes' stream, you have achieved more than an atmosphere of agreement. You have the chairman's permission for six minutes without interruption. You have also shown that your talk has a business-like plan. You have declared your signposts. These provide you with valuable control factors. For instance, you are in the middle of describing a difficult technical point when Sir Charles Thingummy butts in with 'But what's all this going to cost?' Your whole presentation could lose momentum if you let him put a stopper in at this juncture. Your first instinct might be to become defensive and argue with the man. Don't. Your clear signposting now becomes useful. Open your ears not your mouth. Give him your full attention. Listen to his question politely. You then turn to the chairman and say 'Mr Jackson, you will recall that I was coming to the balance sheet under heading three.' Mr Jackson had told you that that was the way he wanted it – 'Yes', he had said. The chairman will respond in one of two ways. He will either say, 'nevertheless, please answer the question now' (you, of course, do so) or he'll say 'Shut up, Charlie. He's coming to the money later.' If the latter response gives you a glow of smug satisfaction that you've beaten Charlie, beware. It could be a Pyrrhic victory. You've made Charlie look a fool. That will not help you. You've got to give the man a ladder to climb down and to restore a good relationship between you – so:

'Thank you, Mr Jackson.' Then, turning to Charlie, 'Yes, I am coming to the money later, Sir Charles. I'm glad you asked. It's probably the most important question of the lot. May I come straight back to you when we get to the finances?'

What does Charlie say? He says, 'Yes, please do', and doesn't feel a fool any more.

You then put in a quick summary to mend the break and get back on line.

But, when you arrive at the money stage, do come straight to Sir Charles. After all, you are both in agreement that this item is vitally important and he'll be grateful you remembered that he was the one who had asked this key question. So start on the balance sheet with your ally, Sir Charles.

To recapitulate on your opening. What? State what the proposal is. Profit early in their minds. Get the yes yes yes stream going. In collaboration with the chairman, establish the signposts and gain control points. Keep it brief. From now on all your steps should be structured to get a 'yes' response.

Why? – an unsuccessful salesman would immediately flourish his product and expound on its virtues – before we see a reason for change. You must first establish their need; what is wrong with the present situation from their point of view. There must be no woolly, abstract statements. Give them the facts. So what is wrong with their present situation? The old machines break down (facts, figures, money), produce faulty goods (facts, figures, money), soak up excessive labour costs (facts, figures, money). The competitors have jumped ahead of us. Market share has shrunk and customer complaints pile up relentlessly (facts, figures, money). The firm is in trouble with safety regulations – or whatever truths will make them see that something has to be done. Their situation is dire. *Facts, figures, proof* must support *everything* you say. Do not assert anything or give opinions. Make the facts speak to them. You will have selected the one, two or three most compelling facts to emphasize – remember no laundry list especially at this stage. Keep it concise. Select. Justify. If some of your main facts can be culled from their own reports, etc. use them – examples close to home. In two or three minutes you should have them groggy, muttering, 'I knew things were bad, but this is awful. All that money going down the drain.'

They must clearly recognize that they are losing or failing to gain one, two, or three major benefits. 'Yes,' they say, 'yes, all this is true! What can we do about it?' They are now conditioned to listen to your solution. Not until they are thus rendered receptive to change will you introduce your scheme.

So that is the *why*. They recognize that they have a *need*.

How? is, of course, how your scheme will solve their problem and produce a profit for them. Here again facts speak louder than opinions. Have the machines been tried under practical conditions? What results from what authoritative tests? What experience have other users had?

Will they fit our floorspace? What happens to the old machines? Scrap or some return on selling them elsewhere? Demonstrate improved product, economy. Show how labour is saved. What other machine have you considered? Why are Gumbils better for us? etc. etc.

In considering other options you show that you are not blinkered and have truly worked to get the best solution for them.

I have based this example on a real proposal. My friends often let me join their meetings, sometimes as an adviser, sometimes as an advocate, sometimes merely to help me to stay away from heady theory and to keep my feet on the ground. I've changed all the names. If there really is a Gumbil machine the makers will, I hope, forgive me.

You will recall that the proposer has made a good professional start and presented the facts showing a need for change: he has also proved that the Gumbil machines best meet their needs. The next heading is *Who?* – people – and in this case the speaker had not sufficiently thought this through. One learns a great deal about speaking by watching the audience, like the psychologist at a strip show. I observed that one of the directors – a short, square man called Armstrong – was becoming squarer and squarer and was obviously building up to an outburst. The outburst duly happened. Armstrong vigorously denounced the proposal. He was so clearly concerned that the presenter was asked to leave. The board did not want a quarrel – that's what it was becoming – in front of one of their managers.

Over a glass before lunch the group chairman, who had presided at the meeting, took me aside.

'Bell', he murmured, 'what did you think of that presentation?'

'I thought it a good case', said I. 'I was surprised to see you throw him out.'

'I thought so too.' Then he added, in that soft, slow voice with a rising inflection that people use when they want something: 'You get on well with Armstrong, don't you?'

'Yes, I do. I admire him very much.'

'I was wondering,' he began. I interrupted:

'If you are going to ask me to find out what's eating him, yes, I will. I'm professionally interested. I was going to ask you whether I might do so.'

Mr Armstrong had left school at the age of fourteen with no advantages except guts and intelligence. Through home study, night school and tremendous effort he had become a fully qualified engineer. He knew the shop floor from hard experience. He was probably the best works director in his field. A great chap. At the right moment, I led him to the question.

'I don't mind telling you,' he growled. 'I've worked damn hard to get where I am. There are about a thousand people in my division. Put these bloody machines in and in a year there'll only be half that. What about my people who are going to lose their jobs? What about me and my job?'

Subsequently, we had tremendous luck with this presentation. The board saw salvation in the Gumbil machines and wanted them. With the full co-operation of the chairman and connivance from the others the case came up again at the next meeting. Armstrong was furious. The chairman summed up the main points of the earlier presentation and then gave the floor to the manager. He rapidly eased into his theme, then added:

'There is a snag here, gentlemen, a serious snag. Mr Armstrong has in his division 1104 people (exact figure that even Armstrong didn't know). If we put these new machines in I estimate that within ten months that division will be reduced to 492 people!' Worse than Armstrong had thought. 'But, Mr Chairman and gentlemen, may I remind you that in thirteen months time, we are losing Mr Christie' – a director sitting near the top of the table. 'Mr Christie has charge of the biggest division in the group and, as we all know, he is retiring. If I may say so, with respect, directors like Mr Christie do not grow on gooseberry bushes. He is going to need some replacing. His successor must be a man who knows the business, knows the firm and knows our people. If we put these machines in we are going to have Mr Armstrong practically unemployed. I know it's none of my business, sir, but I suggest that this might be a very powerful argument in favour of these machines.'

Not a word from Armstrong, but a faint suggestion of 'purr, purr'.

This incident actually happened. It would have been impertinent without the backing of the directors. The manager had been briefed to do this. It worked, and brought forward the board's decision – tacitly already made – that they would in time offer the job to Armstrong.

It was typical of the man that he stubbornly refused to accept the proposal until he could make certain by consultation with the unions and others concerned that no hardship would ensue.

You must not expect such luck. But this case does illustrate a requirement to consider the who. You must not leave out people. Whose budget provides the money? 600 employees redundant or to be resituated. You are affecting many people's livelihood. Here is a headache for the personnel director. The unions won't be amused. Who gains? Who loses? You must think beyond your enthusiasm for your scheme. If there are drawbacks, face them. Find a benefit counterbalancing snags if you can.

Where? – sometimes the where is vital – e.g. more central location, easier deliveries, labour readily available, government grants and so on.

But your strongest point to obtain action as well as agreement is the *When*. If you can show that money is dropping out of their pockets every day, that competitors will be able to jump in if we delay – that the options you have to get immediate delivery of the machines, now in stock, will lapse and that the maker's lead time may be two years if the competitors get there first. The law is already intimating that you are not complying with safety regulations and a closure is on the cards – *urgency* – use it as your final point and make utterly clear what action they need to take to gain the benefits. A compelling *when* is essential if you seek action, now.

Money – here you are probably on ground more familiar to the directors than to you. You are in the temple of Mammon. Money is their god and you never laugh at anyone else's god. So treat money with the greatest respect. No jokes, no light remarks such as 'It's only a couple of hundred thousand'. It's their money you are talking about and no laughing matter. Above all, be accurate in your sums. One slipshod reckoning makes all your other figures suspect. If you are not a money man I recommend that you ask the finance director to discuss the figure with you beforehand. You have to present what is in effect a balance sheet:

This is what they spend, and how.	This is what their profit will be, and how.

Avoid abstract phrases like 'a considerable amount', 'increased sales', etc. How much – in cash? – is what they require. Never make forecasts except as an extrapolation from solid facts. The board will probably want you to give them only the main figures – justified – but you must have exact details available if they ask for them.

At another meeting, a woman personnel manager attempted to obtain £32,000 from a hard-nosed group of director, in order to provide, in the factory grounds, a creche for young mothers. She pleaded sentimentally about the problems these women suffered in coming to work and neglecting their little ones. The board threw her out, muttering imprecations such as 'We're here to make a bit of brass not fork out cash for do-gooders'. They used the phrase 'Do-gooder' in the pejorative sense; but this woman was indeed a doer of good, a wonderful caring woman who believed in her proposal. Later, when I visited her office on another matter, she was still seething with rage and frustration. She fumed:

'Now I suppose we've got to go through the annual rigmarole all over again – every year we get this – we need another 200 women because most of last year's that we took on have left. That means advertising, extra staff to deal with telephones, letters, and interviews, new overalls and things, sorting out their tax and National Insurance, health checks, doctors' time, weeks of training, complaints about scrap and wasted time and effort; supervisors going round the bend – we lost two of them last year because they got the blame for the dud work the new girls turned out. Why are they so pig-headed, these so-called directors?'

'Can you put a cash figure on what you've just told me?' I asked.

'I suppose I could', she replied.

'I suggest that you do two things. First of all make a survey of as many as you can of the women who left, and find out why they did so.'

'I already know about some of them. About eighty are working at Johnson's – that's the factory two bus stops farther away from town – and we've trained them for Johnson's benefit. They've got a nursery already. Also, about a third of them don't want to work a full day. They want to take their older children to school and be back in time to take them home. The others want full time. If Johnson's can do it, why can't we? OK I'll do a survey. Then what do you suggest I do next?'

'Work out what this annual jamboree is costing the directors – every detail – advertising costs, training costs, losing customers, cost of scrap and so on. To be practical, can you allow for a full-time nurse and a roster of mothers doing an hour a day voluntarily? I'll come to see you in three weeks time with my own estimates.'

The personnel manager produced facts and figures. One customer's account had been worth:

4 years ago	£122,000
3 years ago	£105,000
2 years ago	£ 20,000
This year	£nil

Ten other cases were documented. The losses directly attributable to faulty goods and inferior workshop skills amounted to £700,000's worth of business plus annual costs for scrap and replacements, £22,000. Demand still existed but these customers now bought what they wanted from a competitor.

Irrefutable proof came from the accounts, from salesmen's reports, a report from the works manager, supervisors' reports, and a dossier of customers' letters with justified complaints.

Staff turnover included two supervisors, four salesmen and ninety-two from the shop floor who had left for jobs with fewer vexations. Annual costs for recruitment, training, documentation, clothing etc. – £12,750.

Total:	£720,000 – rising
	£ 22,000 – rising
	£ 12,750 – rising
	£754,000 – rising

The personnel manager would not get another hearing from the board. She took the facts privately to the sales director. Four days later the board sent for her.

She got her creche – and a small playground. She had all

the aces – their need, their greed and their status as good employers. The figures astonished the board. In business facts have more power than sentiment.

A medical friend of mine had a problem. He worked in a poor inner-city area and wanted to buy the house next door to his surgery so that he could take a partner and expand his practice. But he, too, was struggling and hoped to gain the support of the local council in buying the house. Early sounding indicated that he hadn't a chance. Because he bathed and shaved every day and wore a suit – even a necktie – and ran his own business, the local councillors wrote him off as a bloated capitalist. Not that the councillors were less than profligate with the ratepayers' money. Had they not supported the Arts? Why, only last week they had given a fellow with matted hair and grubby toes peeping through green sandals £2,000 for a masterpiece consisting of a heap of bricks surmounted by a plastic dog turd. To hell with the rich!

So how could the doctor chisel through their prejudices and apply need, greed and status to his proposal? His personal need would carry no weight whatever: so this must not be put forward. There was no monetary gain for them. The key to use here was their self-esteem, to feed their exalted opinion of themselves, to bring them renown. And votes.

The doctor described the conditions in the waiting room, waiting being the operative word. Sometimes patients would have to queue for hours. The narrow room lacked space for enough seating and there was an undeniable risk that children with notifiable diseases could infect others. He dwelt on this point, quoting two well-authenticated cases, one in America and one in Britain, where such squalid contact started epidemics and where the local health authorities were held to blame. He developed several specific examples of poorer patients receiving less than their due and children suffering. Complaints grew every day and most of them were directed at them, the local authority. You will see the theme line and its possibilities.

The council gave the doctor a generous grant to develop a Medical Health Centre (the councillors loved that sort of phrase) and in a glow of self-satisfaction provided him not only with the house but the means to engage more staff and to do his job properly. The local newspapers mentioned almost all the councillors, with photographs, and the mayor enjoyed the glory of opening the new establishment with a plaque in the waiting room displaying his name.

Vanity. The point is surely made by now that you must work on other people's vanity, their self-concern. If you let your own egocentricity focus inwards nobody sympathizes: they have their own, to them, much more interesting, problems. Therefore, in seeking agreement, fulfil their need if you can. Appealing to their greed is not so pleasant and puffing up their self-importance a sickening last resort.

But they all work.

Exercise

Structure a case presentation, real or imaginary, using the questions (page 52) as guidelines and as a checklist. Take an hour on the broad outline. You'll need more time and spadework to obtain and to verify your facts.

NOTES

5 Specialist talk

John Logie Baird's discovery of the principles of television was useless; Einstein helped nobody with his thinking on relativity nor did Fleming with penicillin until they made their facts and theories known to other people. Knowledge locked away in the recesses of a single mind has little value before other minds receive the key and gain access to it. Many specialists believe that their work stops when they have uncovered the facts. A question was asked of them. They worked on it, investigated it thoroughly and found the answer. And that, they say, is the end of their job. But is it?

Industrial concerns employ scientists, accountants and other specialists in order to obtain from them information and expert guidance towards profitable action. Yet although specialists study and sweat for five, ten, fifteen, twenty years, a lifetime, to equip themselves as experts they rarely study the techniques of passing their hard-gained information to other people.

Have you ever wondered why so many speakers on religious matters ooze superiority and make us feel some sort of lesser breed: why they are so tight-lipped, frigid and grim? Is it because they agree with the tabloid newspapers that good news is no news and that sin is much more juicy and interesting? They are supposed to be spreading the Gospel. Gospel means good news. That, surely, is something to be happy about. Such men have the wrong attitude to their listeners – and to their message.

One occasionally meets specialists who could well bear this in mind. They fit an accepted definition of an expert as: X – an unknown quantity; spurt – a drip under pressure.

As a specialist you must counter this calumny by maintaining that you offer a service when presenting the results of your labours and that it is usually good news. Also, you know more about your special subject than do outsiders. You have the facts.

A young man at a gathering which included several clergymen asked to be excused because he was going to the races with a well-known journalist. His father was upbraided by a bishop for allowing his son to associate with such a deplorable man, a confidence trickster – a tipster! The youth in defence of his friend said:

'Doug Galley (the tipster) studies the horse's form and his past running, the jockeys, the weights, the going, all the other horses in the race, the trainers, everything on record, and, on those facts, bases his forecast that his selection will win. Tonight, everyone can look at the papers and find out whether he tipped a winner. You, on the other hand, forecast everlasting life and glory and all that jazz. You haven't a single fact to go on. No one ever comes back from the dead to prove you right or wrong. So who's the confidence trickster?' Then he added: 'So long, Dad. You're welcome to this bunch of guess men' and departed hurriedly.

Facts are the rock on which the status of a specialist is founded. You are not guess men. We rely on you to know about matters beyond our reach. And we trust you. Whether you are an engineer, a scientist, or any other qualified specialist you've had to work hard and long to achieve such distinction. But, with distinction often comes separation, even reclusion. As an anchorite retires to his cell, so do some specialists go deeper and deeper into their exclusive world. They get to know more and more about less and less until, like the fabulous oozle bird, they fly backwards in gradually diminishing circles until they disappear up their own rectum. Not you, of course. You know that 'no man is an island unto himself'. Even the greatest of minds have little value until other people can understand and use their thoughts. Specialists are important people who have the talent, the training and the patience to investigate matters that we cannot. If they keep their findings to themselves, however, of what use are they? Nobody pays a salary to Robinson Crusoe – genius or not.

Personal skills in communicating information should be an integral part of every degree course. Alas, no students are more neglected in this respect than technical and scientific people. You may protest, sir, but thousands, yearly, come into industry and commerce without a notion of how to present, orally, either themselves or their results. The specialist has more problems with speaking than the layman, the principal difficulty being that he must avoid at all costs merely transferring the problems to his listeners.

You already know how to tackle a speaking job in general, but you don't offer 'caviar to the general' unless you develop their taste for it as it is, or make it more palatable for them. In your world, you are vastly superior to the rest of us but there must be no feeling that you are coming down to our level; rather that you are raising us toward yours. Even with a totally lay audience you are not addressing fools. They have their own values. During a speaking workshop with a highly qualified group, a huge Rolls-Royce glided past the window carrying a bag of golf clubs and one of the directors. It was a glorious day and the scientists were loud in the condemnation of the director – 'Here are we sweating away etc., etc.,'. Later, I reproved the director for his lack of tact. He asked me to apologize to the scientists, who nevertheless continued to gnash their teeth. Two days later, the director asked: 'Bell, have you still got that bunch of technical blokes with you?'

'Yes', I replied. 'They are a splendid group and I hope you are still suitably chastened.'

'Well', he grinned, smugly, 'ask them to buy the Evening Argus tonight. On the front page they'll see that we're building a new plant and taking on 400-odd people. That Monday afternoon on the golf course, I arranged to borrow seventeen million quid to make it possible. Ask those eggheads if any of them could have done that.'

You might have a roomful of people such as that director to address, all of whom may be experts in their own line but ignorant about other matters. Most of us have vast empty spaces in our knowledge even of truly elementary things like how do you make a major chord into a minor?, what is an active verb?, is energy the same as force?, what is the capital of Bulgaria?, who is the Minister of the Environment?, what does grunth mean?, and, something you use every day, where and what is a hypothalamus? Ignorant, that's what we all are in everybody else's sphere but our own. So have mercy. Remember it took you years and a lot of sweat to learn even the basics of your expertise. Don't throw us a bone unless we have the teeth to deal with it. As obvious as it is to you, you might have to establish A, B and C before we can understand your ingenious thoughts on D, E and F. You can never develop something completely new unless you relate it to what people already know. And this is the key to your success as a presenter of esoteric data – a comprehensive study of your audience. With an audience fully qualified in your subject you might be able to start at rung six on a ten-rung ladder. Even with them, a few reminders might not come amiss. Quite rightly, you may suggest that such advice should be unnecessary. It's so obvious.

An organization devoted to the interests of qualified

engineers asked me to talk one evening about communications. I accepted the invitation with pleasure, drafted an outline of the talk, then handed my notes to a colleague who is a member, asking for his observations.

'Fine', he said. 'Fine – if they are all engineers.'

'But, this is the organization for . . . Surely they are all qualified engineers?'

'Sometimes they invite people from other disciplines.'

I telephoned the Secretary and arranged to call on him and have a chat about the talk. In reply to my question he said: 'Oh, no. They will not all be engineers. This is a special occasion. They are bringing guests who will be chemists, physicists, geologists, people of all sorts. And their wives and friends will come with them.'

The talk had to be entirely restructured. We had a successful evening. As I was departing, the Secretary, after thanking me, said:

'You know, Mr Bell, we've had some ghastly evenings here. Some of the speakers talked high above the heads of the audience; some below their knees.' Then he added: 'I've been in this job fifteen years and you are the first speaker who has taken the trouble to visit me to find out about the audience, the first and the only one.'

Sometimes the obvious is unseen. Reconnaissance pays. Without it you'll be like the fellow who did a high dive into six inches of water.

Often, during a lunchtime discussion with a group of technical people, the tablecloth serves as a sketch pad. Explanatory diagrams sprawl all over it. This is because some people find it easier to think in action and when they can see what they are talking about. For this reason, another method of brainstorming might appeal to you. Instead of jotting down a review of your subject in note form, try standing up with a blank sheet of flip chart paper on your desk. Write your subject heading in a box in the centre and get every possibility out of your mind and on to the chart.

KING ALFRED R. NAVY
OTTAR EXPLORED
ESQIMAUX LIFE
FISHERIES WHALES
BASES FOR START POINT
LOCAL SEAS
WEATHER
WHAT ASSUMED
SEAGOING NATIONS
FOOD
DEFENCE
KNOWLEDGE
AIDS TO
LAY-MONEY MEN
WHAT ASSUMED
DETAILS
EARLY NAVIGATORS
MODERN
SHIPWRECKS
INSURANCE
ALASKA – OIL
BARENTS – LABRADOR CURRENT
AUDIENCE
FELLOW SPECIALISTS
WHAT THEY CONTRIB. TO STATE OF THE ART.
VELOCITY OF CURRENTS / S
+ DEEP TI
NAVIGATIO
HERODO
HUMBOLT
POLITICS
WAR.
GRAND BANKS
NAUTILUS
SADKO DRIFT
PLEASURES
SPORTS
SHIPS
TRANSPOR
GLACIATION
PAST & PRESENT
RIDGE THULE
BENJ. FRANKLIN
PHANTOM BOTTOMS
PACIFIC
GULF STREAM
DEPTHS
SALTIEST
COMMERCE
FISH – WHE
WHY
EPICENTRES
ARCTIC ROSS ANT-ARC
AMUNDSEN SCOTT.
ATLANTIC
ATLANTIS
PLATO
GREAT BANK
GLACIERS
HOW FORMED
WHEN – OCEAN VS GREEK
AUSTRALASIA
THE OCEANS AND THE SEAS
BIBLICAL SOURCES OF INFO.
MEDITERRANEAN
RED SEA AEGEA
MINDANOA TRENCHES
MARINE LIFE
DEVELOPMENT
DEPOSITS
PACIFIC – EARTHQUAKES
VOLCANOES
STASSFURT SALT BEDS
SCRIPPS INST OF O'OGRAPHY
PERMIAN PERIOD
DEPTHS
EQUATORIAL CURRENTS
POLYNESIANS CORAL
KON-TIKI
JAPAN
TUSCARORA
UNDERSEA MOUNTAINS
SALT LAKE
ISLANDS
FATHOGRAMS, CONTOURS, FL
TOF
DYNOMOMETER
IND. OCEAN
E. INDIES – TIMOR
CAPE HORN . — S. AROUND
ETC.

Figur

Make ideas grow upon ideas, concept upon concept, each one sparking off others – not necessarily in any logical order; just aim for a review of the whole subject. You will find all sorts of options opening up and you may need several sheets. Keep your audience in mind. Work at speed. (Please see Figure 7.)

In designing the structure of your talk, your knowledge of report writing can be adapted to an oral presentation. You would probably shape a written report on the traditional headings:

1 Cover, title page – first impressions.
2 Busy man's page, executive summary, in-a-nutshell version of what follows, mostly for laymen. Table of contents – brief. Signposts.
3 Introduction. The object and reason for the work. Background might need to be established, filled in and, sometimes, explained.
4 Methodology. Certainly your fellow-specialists will want to know how you tackled the job – what apparatus, what tests, to what tolerances you worked. What authority for:
5 Results, facts and figures. Graphs, charts etc. – visual aids.
6 A firm clear summary highlighting the main facts.
7 Conclusions. So what?
8 Recommendations. What do you want us to do? What do you want us to take away in our minds? The afterglow. Impact at ending.

You will know that items 1, 2 and 6 are better deferred until you have decided on the main body. Please refer to earlier chapters to check that you are applying the basic principles of the P stage and stage three.

Speaking for the specialist takes many forms. You may be making a presentation to a board to gain financial support for your department or the development of new techniques. You might be making a sales-support presentation; giving a lecture or reading a paper to fellow specialists: explaining matters to manufacturers and other laymen in your discipline. You are comfortable in your own professional knowledge but the extra dimension of being a first class communicator must also be part of your persona. Maybe you have it already, in which case you will know that it is mostly horse-sense with the blinkers removed.

A scientist seeking board approval for a scheme rambled in his own world for twenty minutes and left the room, by request. As the door closed, one of the directors declared: 'That man must be a genius. I didn't understand a bloody word he said'.

One can have little sympathy with that scientist. If he is old enough and intelligent enough to gain a doctorate there is no excuse for his being incomprehensible.

As for the blunt director, he is almost unlettered – none after his name and few in his mind; but he is the man who can say yes or no to a proposal. Frequently, this sort of man bristles at the mere thought of college boys. Sometimes he is envious of their superiority and hates their display of it. But is a specialist really superior if, when he could make the point by saying 'Tests proved that the handle gets too hot', he blathers, instead, that 'The results of a period of *ad hoc* experimentation, supplemented by both statistical analysis and consideration of empirical factors thought to be universally viable in the context of the areas in which utilization could be expected to approach a maximum, indicated that the thermal conductivity of that portion of the equipment designed for prehensile digital contact was such as to present a surface whose temperatures would markedly exceed the generally accepted threshold of sensory discomfort – etcetera, etcetera, etcetera.'

Why do so many technicians, trained in logic and

precision, write and speak such twaddle? Is it because they are suspicious of the arts, afraid that what they do might lose mystique? Or is it that they cannot bother to bring logic and precision into their use of language? Many a brilliant young man, on reaching middle age, wonders what went wrong with his career. Let him re-read some of his papers. The answers could be found in them, and every speech a coffin nail.

In any large organization roughly one-third of the people over the age of twenty-eight are dead. By this time they have accumulated enough cliché phrases and routine attitudes to lean on until their pensions turn up. There seems to be no reason for them to think any more. It is enough just to react according to the rule book and the jargon – 'It must be pointed out that in view of the fact that . . .' 'The conceptual philosophy of commonality and standardization at this point in time could be said to have, perhaps, groundings in feasibility which, with the basic assumption that . . .' '. . . the viability of these parameters, shiftwise . . .'. All non-think stuff, torture for the listener and highly dangerous for the specialist.

Danger? What danger? We live in a sea of words. What is wrong with drifting along in the fashionable waters, swallowing the stuff and regurgitating it into the faces of our fellows? Why not? It's easier than thinking.

What happens to a muscle that gets no exercise? It becomes flabby. What happens to a machine that lies idle for years? It becomes rusty and useless. What happens to a brain that does nothing but gather verbal cobwebs? Adult thinking is impossible without a language or some other set of symbols that label the elements we develop into thoughts. If words, for instance, are the bricks and mortar with which we build the wall of thought, does it not follow that the sort of words we habitually use is the sort of thinker we are? Near-enough words, that'll-do words, other people's tired old clichés provide neither keep fit exercise nor nourishment for an active mind. A factory girl whose eight-hour day consists of fitting component A into component B and endlessly repeating the dreary process to feed some production line would go mad if she thought about it very much. So she works mechanically and dreams of her boyfriend or of being a duchess. But this will not do for expensively trained specialists.

Your language, technical language, has the advantage of being clearly defined, every word of it. Used properly, it assists constructive thought and communication among those who understand it. Abused, or flaunted because you want to imply that you are superior to people outside 'the club', it can cause trouble – for you as much as for your victims. The English language provides one of the most precise, subtle, flexible and vigorous aids to clear thought and effective presentations. No specialist can claim to be more than half-baked if he does not learn how to control it.

If you feel that I am being a little hard on the specialist please accept that such severity is founded on my deep admiration and respect for those of you who have taken such pains to rise above the ordinary. It is infuriating to see qualified people receiving less appreciation than the glossy boys.

Effective speaking is an essential element in your professional life. You have so much to offer and what you offer should be easy to understand, and to accept. You above all people must command attention. But you must use the language of the audience or explain your own. Please adjust your language before speaking.

Presenting a paper

This is potentially one of the most dismal of occasions because both you and the audience are caught between two stools. Is it a speech or is it a reading? You will be required to follow the normal practices of the organizing body. Was the paper sent out in advance for the members to study? Or are they receiving the information for the first time, now, at your presentation? Is yours the only paper on this day? Have you a time limit? How much time, if any, will be allowed for questions and discussions? You will of course insist on full information about the composition of the audience.

Let us be selfish for a while and consider this occasion as an opportunity to increase your personal stature as a specialist. The following method has been helpful to several of my friends. In essence, what you do is to prepare two presentations.

First, prepare a speech or lecture using all the advantages of a full stage and equipment. Please re-read the earlier chapter on preparation and follow the procedures for building a first class talk.

First, gather and scan material. Go through every document – your original briefing – all your log books, bench notes, correspondence, references. Trace the whole project from its birth to its present state of maturity. (This part of the exercise will give you added power at question time.) Note everything and check facts. You may be surprised at how much detail you had forgotten. Then proceed to stages two and three. Not until you know that you could, if required, make a thoroughly professional oral presentation should you attempt to write your paper. Even go so far as to present the talk to a few colleagues.

Second, writing the paper should be comparatively easy for you now. You have the whole scope and shape clear in your mind. Your language will be more human and you will have an audience more firmly in your sights than is usual at a reading. It may surprise you to find that the oral structure adds strength to your paper. On the day, your delivery becomes real communication with flesh-and-blood people instead of a lonely monologue. I hope you have the time to try this method. Your listeners will certainly be grateful. You will experience a surer command of your subject and increase your own confidence. Reading a paper need not be a dismal affair, especially if you can escape from the lectern occasionally and speak to us directly.

A sales-support presentation

Until recently, one could easily offend, say, a research chemist by suggesting that he was part of the company's sales force. Modern specialists have more sense. They know that everyone from the switchboard operator to the chairman have one end in view – to satisfy customers and to keep the money rolling in. And who is more important to the achievement of this objective than the specialist? The salesman is the fellow at the sharp end. He bears the brunt of the customers' displeasure if the goods are shoddy, the price too high and if nobody gives him anything new and superior to sell.

The salesman hasn't got a chance without you, e.g. a man selling insurance without the backing of an actuary; a seller of power stations without the physicist, the engineer, the economist, the ecologist, the lawyer; a shop assistant selling clothing without the textile specialist and the dyestuff chemist in support. Look around any food shop. There one sees evidence of expertise not only in the processing of foodstuffs but also the part played by packaging, metallurgists, plastics, paint; air conditioners, computer people et al. Science and technology are no longer closet skills; they are out in the vulgar world.

Some companies use technical representatives in the field, but these men do tend to lose touch with the research and development department. The engineering side of a presentation has more validity if the engineer speaks for it. A specialist who is also an effective speaker is not only a rare bird, he is a jewel in the crown. As a specialist, know your place in a sales presentation. It is mighty important. So are you.

You must work closely with the representative. He knows the customers' needs and their quirks and, in many respects, is better informed than you are. Agree on the scope and the limits of your part in the proceedings. Concentrate on your own presentation and leave the rest to him. Use speaking disciplines in your preparation. You will be expected to answer all questions as an authority. You can learn a lot from direct customer reaction and take it back to the drawing board to your own advantage.

There are still a few specialists who resent being associated with sales. If they are self-sufficient and self-financing well and good. The phrase 'it's a small world' was coined for them. But a specialist who is affronted by being asked to take part in a sales presentation loses an opportunity for giving a service and for self-development.

The lecture

For many people the word 'lecture' has unhappy connotations such as reproach or censure, a dressing down. To students it often means boredom, a suspension of life, a plague to be endured. At a certain university, Professor Bland empties the lecture hall with monotonous regularity. At the lectures of his colleague, Professor Vital, the same hall is packed, standing-room only – and lucky to get that.

Professor Bland received what we call all the advantages – well-to-do parents, an income of his own, the best of prep schools, the best of public schools and thence to the university of Unamit. He enjoyed the life there and, after graduation, slid easily into a comfortable rut as an academic unsullied by experience outside its ivy-clad walls. He writes papers, has even had books published (at his own expense – a procedure known in the book trade as vanity publication). With great charm he entertains a select coterie which does not include the plebs. His students he tolerates as the price of Utopia. Lectures are simple for him; he merely reads one of his papers. His influential connections keep him safe.

One day he will become a white-haired, pink-faced institution and they'll give him a grand retirement dinner, maybe a title.

Bland makes no secret of his contempt for Professor Vital. 'Oh, Vital is very popular. After all he is famous as a broadcaster and gives the students a show – he should be at the Palladium.'

Vital is in demand as a broadcaster because he is, first, a thoroughly informed academic. His enthusiasm and passionate curiosity about his speciality create a blast of fresh air in dusty corners and invigorate the minds of his listeners. He is not a tea party man, but give him a fistful of earth or a couple of beetles and he opens up a new world for us. He sometimes works for months researching and preparing for an hour's presentation. That is why everything he does makes us feel that he has just come across a fascinating bit of knowledge and he wants us to share it with him.

We have a choice, the cloister or the lusty world that real people live in. Your lecture should be an exhilarating event. Nothing in life is without interest and excitement – unless we make it so.

Words

Speakers often complain that they have plenty of ideas but cannot find the words to express them. They assert that their problem is a limited vocabulary. This is rarely the truth; the real trouble is that they have not yet clarified their thoughts. Thought processes are so closely related to words or symbols that they are almost inseparable. Look around, wherever you are, and get a general impression of what you see. Now look around a second time – and think about what you see.

Did you find, second time round, that you were using words such as table, chair, curtains, window, books, in your living room? Or, in the garden, words like trees, magnolia, cabbage, grass, dog, pigeon? Try again please. Try to elucidate and to fix a thought without using labels of some sort. Difficult, isn't it? But once you have the thought clear, the words are already in place. People with English as a mother tongue are lucky because usually only one word is the right one – there are few absolute synonyms. Top, cover, flap, bonnet, dome, cap, protector, roof, hood, lid – all convey the same broad idea but only one of them is exact for your precise thought. You would not agree that 2 + 2 = 4.001. It's near enough but it will not do; neither will near-enough words. They lead to near-enough thinking.

If you mean 'he waved goodbye' don't say 'he made an undulating valedictory gesture'. Which brings us to posh words, swank. A man wrote to me asking for a job. His letter contained a dozen windbag phrases including the information that he had 'acquired a plenitude of impeachable references.' He did not get the job.

Speakers are sometimes tempted to show off. Resist such temptation. Clear thoughts can usually be conveyed to an audience in simple language. The specialist is at risk in using specialist language to a lay audience, but at least his technical words are officially defined. He means what he says – although it might leave us no wiser unless he interprets his language. Far greater hazards for the unwary are vogue words and phrases – heard, picked up and used without thought because it is believed that they will impress. 'Now' becomes 'at this point in time'; 'soon' becomes 'in the not too far distant future' – two simple ones to start with: I'm sure you can make your own list. Refuse to gather verbal flab. Keep your mind alive. Present your own ideas in your own way. Don't worry about words. Get the thought clear and words will look after themselves.

A novelist weaves words to evoke situations in our minds, and each reader makes his own mental pictures, coloured by his personal experience and imagination. An undertaker doesn't see a funeral with the eyes of a widow;

but such variation matters little so long as they are both swept along by the story in their own way – and at their own pace. A speaker needs to be more direct. Every mind in the audience must grasp each point as it is delivered – at the pace of the speaker – or lose it. One sure way of sending their thoughts off at a tangent is to indulge in abstractions.

If you ask the members of a group to draw a picture when you say (one at a time) four words, the results are predictable. For 'dog' they will sketch a dog: for 'book' they will sketch a book. But, for 'capability', no two people will produce the same sketch; neither will they for 'development' or any other abstract noun. A listener more easily matches his thought to yours if you use concrete words. He will conjure up any thought he likes in response to an abstract word. Beware of abstractions. They are the harlots of language and can seduce you into doing things you shouldn't. They can disguise sloppy thinking or even replace thought altogether. Politicans love them when they have their mouths open and nothing in their minds but to re-process the party clap-trap. Pseudo-intellectuals stand naked stripped of their polysyllables. If you ask a poseur what he means by an abstraction he will try to fob you off by using six others equally vague, a sure sign that he is bogus. Like cigarettes, abstractions become a habit and bad for your mental health. The easiest test for your language as a speaker is: 'Would I say it like that to my wife or to a couple of friends or to my colleagues at work?'

Speaking is probably the oldest form of human communication. It is certainly the most natural to modern man, but unless other minds can process or use what is said, speaking is just a useless shifting of wind. 'Though I speak with the tongues of men and of angels, and have not charity, I am become as sounding brass or a tinkling cymbal.'

Exercises

1 Take any ten specialist words in your discipline and try to interpret each one so that a layman would clearly understand.

2 Shape a fifteen-minute talk to fellow specialists about your current work.

3 Prepare a case to your board for an expensive piece of new equipment.

6 One to one talk

Interview. The word divides into two parts, inter and view – two people taking a look at each other, examining the facts and between them deciding on some agreed action. On the face of it, the job interview appears to be weighted on the side of the one recruiting; the sales interview on the side of the buyer; the disciplinary interview on the side of the boss. But is this necessarily so? Both sides want something. If you are a candidate for a job, the interviewer wants you to demonstrate that his search is over and that he has got the right man. You, of course, want the job and he has to satisfy you that you are selling your services profitably.

A personnel manager has the advantage of much greater experience in a recruitment interview. He will have devised a system to grade the candidates. Their application forms or letters provide him with some knowledge of the background of each applicant and he has probably eliminated most of them without interview. This is a valuable point for the candidate. He has already got to first base against competition. The interviewer has worked out questions requiring answers. The candidate must anticipate these questions and also prepare some of his own. A good interviewer will do his best during the early stages to put the candidate at ease. He will more fully explain the job and the conditions. The intelligent candidate will listen without interrupting and perhaps reshape some of the questions he has in mind by linking them with the manager's own remarks. It shows that you were paying attention. At some stage, the manager will ask whether there is something more you wish to know about the job. This is your opportunity to show your interest in the company and to clarify conditions from your point of view. Remember, both of you are buying – he buys a service he needs and your talents buy the job. Keep inter and view in your mind. It's a two-way process.

At a disciplinary interview the sensible boss wants you to go back to work without continuing the behaviour that caused him to have you on the carpet. You both have something to gain – or to lose.

A short course in management communications

The seven most important words:
  I am sorry. I made a mistake.
The six most important words:
  Let us examine the facts, together.
The five most important words:
  You did a good job.
The four most important words:
  What is your opinion?
The three most important words:
  If you please.
The two most important words:
  Thank you.
The one most important word:
  You.
The least important word – I.

At a sales interview the buyer must do his best for his

firm, but he must buy. That's his job. Your job as a salesman is to fulfil his needs. That's your job.

How often have you sat through a tedious lecture or a technical presentation with your brain in torment and your spirits sinking into your boots? It could be worse: you might be a professional buyer – all day and every day on the receiving end of guff and gab. The buyer comes into contact – sometimes conflict – with many types of salesmen. There are those who try to impress him by force; those who plead with him; those who trick him; those who would bribe him; and those who influence him to agree – and to buy.

A buyer's prayer

> 'Hear me, I beseech thee, oh Lord. This day, seven different companies have invited me to welcome their representatives. They will each make what they call a presentation. Pity me, oh Lord.
>
> Will they talk about me and my problems and my needs? No, they will not. Instead they will extol themselves and their products as if I had not heard it all before. Their mouths will move, strange words will emerge and oblige me to regret that I have not had the time to take a degree course in their speciality. Thou knowest that I am a simple man. Their language is not mine; but I do make the decisions. How can I look on them with favour if they speak not to me but to themselves, about themselves and for themselves?
>
> The time is eight minutes after nine of the clock. In perhaps five minutes the Jacobson representative will burst in, red-faced, loaded like a camel and blaming the rest of the world for his not being here at nine, his appointed hour. He is ever late. He will bestrew my desk with impedimenta and samples of goods which I can obtain elsewhere. My secretary will enter soon with a pre-arranged falsehood (pardon me, oh Lord)

that the managing director requires my immediate presence. Goodbye, Mr Rep. Rush to your next call. I expect you are late already.

Oh, Lord, is it not reasonable to expect salesmen to arrive two minutes before and not ten minutes after their appointments?

I am grateful, oh Lord, that my next caller is punctual. He is potentially a good salesman, but his director has no time, he declares, to develop this young man's talents. His apparel is sharp as are his eyes, his manner and his talk. Somebody should tell him, however, that you never win an argument with a customer; that you must never make your customer feel that you believe him to be below your level, not so bright and knowing as you are. To be one up with a customer is often to be two down and sometimes out. But it is not my place to tell him that a good salesman has two eyes, two ears and only one mouth. The mouth is the enemy of the sale when used before the eyes and the ears have done their work.

One of thy creations, oh Lord, a female of the species, calls each week. Thou hast endowed her with ample good looks but she disagrees with thy judgement in that she gilds not only the lily but her hair: but 'tis not gold, 'tis brass. The eyebrows thou gavest her she has plucked out and substituted a hard, thin line of pigment. Her manner is false and her body equally so. Even a simple man such as I can recognize, shall we say, augmentation, when 'tis overdone. She bestows upon me nods and becks and wreathed smiles more suitable for the boudoir than for my office. I could not buy much from such a dolly; my staff would suspect the worst.

A name has been crossed off my list of appointments. It belongs to a fellow who promised me three weeks ago to deliver certain samples and prices, within a few days. When he does call, he will no doubt offer every routine excuse – but only to my secretary. I am no longer available. I am a customer and neglect drives me elsewhere. Woe is me!

What's that? What did you say, God? You're fed up with my lamentations and why don't I just tell them briefly how to treat a buyer? Yes. Yes. I will – at once.'

An interview is a case presentation to obtain agreement and action. Agreement means that both sides gain, not just you. Your job is to emphasize what the other party gains. (See Figure 8.)

Figure 8

You cannot achieve this state of his mind unless you have done your homework on him. You must fully understand your customer's problems. You know your own product and you should know the competitor's product at least as well as the buyer does. He may have seen the competitor already and have him in his mind for comparison. Be ready for questions. Sell the difference or rather don't sell. Let him buy and feel that he's made a shrewd deal. Get action, or at least one step of advancement before you go. Make every visit a plus by getting to know more each time about your customer and his needs. Be worthy of his trust. Never let him down. Be punctual and encourage him to talk. Listen. Deal honestly with any reservation he might have. An objection neglected festers like a boil on the neck – and eventually bursts into a mess.

An encounter across a desk can often make or break a career. Failure follows almost inevitably if you present your ideas at the wrong time or if you insist on pushing a proposal from your own point of view.

By all means be relaxed before you go in to win your point, or before the other fellow calls on you. Do your homework. Get your purpose clear. Have your facts ready. Know his viewpoint in relation to your suggestion and start the discussion on the basis of his problems. Until you have established his problems and have shown that you understand them and are in sympathy with them, you must not try to sell him anything. You want him to react, to say 'Yes'. He will not react in your favour if you spend your time putting yourself across. Try it the other way round. Put him and his problems in the forefront. If what you have to sell solves his problems, he'll agree – and buy.

Exercises

1 If your own company has a purchasing department, arrange to sit in with the buyer for, say, one hour each week and, subsequently, once a month. You will learn much about selling.
2 Take one of your customers and write a full analysis of his problems – strictly from his point of view.
3 Do the same for a new prospect. (Do not give solutions: only their problems.)
4 As a personnel manager, prepare a detailed job specification for a key job in your organization and write the

advertisement for the vacancy. Devise a method to grade the applicants and plan the interviews to follow.

5 You are a candidate for an advertised job (study today's newspapers). Get to know all you can about the company. Add twenty per cent to your current salary and prepare a case demonstrating that they need look no further to fill the post. Face facts both for and against yourself.

INCONTINENCE SUFFERERS ANNUAL DINNER

7 Social speaking

Man is as much a territorial creature as are the birds and the beasts, not only in physical terms but also in enclaves of thought, habits, customs and class. Our roots and parentage persist whatever we do later in life. Why does the chairman of a large industrial organization turn to the sports pages to see how Rotherham United fared on Saturday? He hasn't seen them play since he was ten, but he was born there. The Court Circular provides daily interest to some people, but to others, for all they care, it could be a theatre-in-the-round. We all change our outer skins every twenty-seven days but underneath we are what we are. A first class speaker doesn't talk to skin. He goes for the heart and mind not the pretensions.

Social occasions are tribal matters. Whether we speak at a family affair such as a wedding, a business dinner, or a royal banquet, it is a gathering of some sort of clan, a group having a common aim and a definable set of attitudes. As a speaker on such occasions you have one simple purpose; to give pleasure. What will make your audience purr? What will cause them to cry 'Hear! Hear!'? What will make them laugh? What will make them proud that they belong to this club, this lodge, this church, this company, this band of people brought together with a common cause? What sentiment will bring a lump into their throats? What will make them say afterwards 'Oh, I did enjoy that'?

Deliver the answers to these questions and they will be glad that you spoke, especially as you delivered with obvious affection for them, and warm appreciation of their values; and you did so without going on and on and on. Work out a good line to end your speech and do not separate it by too long a time from your first class opening line.

In a social talk at, say, a wedding or a club dinner, your job is to make everyone there feel good, to show them that they are special people, to stimulate in them a glowing pride that they belong to this particular group and that what they do – and are doing – has significance and charm. You cannot overdo genuine appreciation of what is good and true about them. The technique of social speaking consists almost entirely of finding a hard core of sentiment and surrounding it with candy floss. So study your audience. If you do not know enough about them and their achievements, find out at once. It is too late to do so when you are on your feet speaking.

The guests want your talk to be a success. Of course they do. They are on your side. Nobody demands or even expects great oratory on such occasions; but they are giving you their time and attention, so give them a fair exchange. You cannot do this properly if you haven't done your homework and developed a strong feeling of geniality towards them. So enjoy the pleasure of their company, positively, and let them delight in the pleasure of yours.

If you've had the luck to hear the brilliant Bob Monkhouse, after dinner, or Janet Brown who so skilfully slips a clever impression or two into her speeches, or the agreeable Brian Johnston warming the cockles of our hearts, do appreciate that it took years of hard work and experience – and they still work hard at it – to give us so much pleasure. They make it look easy. But don't deceive yourself. It isn't. Unless you are a professional stand-up comedian, don't try to be one. Be genial and good humoured and let both of these qualities run like a thread through your talk. Jokes – 'that reminds me of the one about . . .' – can be your downfall unless they stem naturally from the general flow.

What is funny about these phrases?

'– is the white man's Purdon'
'– a nick in time stops crime'
'– she did – twice!'
'– so bow down, boys, bow down'

There is nothing intrinsically funny about any of them yet these speakers had their audiences roaring with laughter and applause. They were the punch lines of in-jokes and funny only to the insiders who could appreciate the references. Family jokes, club jokes, show that you have this particular audience firmly in your mind and they will appreciate your sharing their humour with them. There must be no spite, nothing which causes pain or embarrassment. The victims should be leading the laughs.

Let us look at two horrible examples so that you can say at the end of each 'What a dreadful man. What an oaf. I would never do a thing like that' – and mean it.

We are at a wedding. One of the families has been established in the Midlands for generations; the other, military stock, always on the move. Both would describe themselves as middle class. The Best Man rises to speak. He is a fellow subaltern in the groom's regiment, and tipsy. He starts with a grubby joke and perceives no warning from the ensuing silence. He rattles on about how well he knows the groom and laughingly describes in colourful detail their drunken escapades with the floozies of the world, not even stopping at the brothel door. The bride, white-faced, was completely unprepared for the information that her new husband had had an abortive affair with one of the bridesmaids and that she herself had been courted on the rebound. The Best Man's father grabbed his ghastly son and threw him out, but too late to prevent life-long damage to the marriage and to both families.

In that incident you will recognize several of the don'ts about social speaking. Where was the Best Man's focus? On himself and his reflected glory from being an intimate of the groom. Does one speak better when fortified by a few drinks? No. When the wine is in the wit is out. Had the oaf prepared? No. He regarded himself as a personality and could do it off the cuff without bothering to prepare. Two minutes' sober thought would have prevented such stupidity.

The objective of speeches at a wedding is to bring delight to the parties joining in the tribal merger, especially to the happy couple. Fathers, mothers, aunts and uncles, cousins and friends – from both families – rarely all meet together except at weddings. Look for the best on both sides and work on that as your dominant theme. Happiness is what you are aiming for. Hit your target. Blessed are the matchmakers. Give them all the help you can.

It is comparatively easy to spot other people's errors and to learn from them, but much more salutary to be made aware of the beam in one's own eye; and to learn from its painful removal. I am the oaf in this example.

We are at the Savoy Hotel in London; the occasion, the annual dinner of a well-known London club. The youthful Bell has been asked to propose the toast of Our Guests of Honour, a famous actress and a cabinet minister. In preparing my speech, the lady presented no difficulty. I knew her well and admired her only just 'on this side idolatory'. She had graced some of my scripts and given immense pleasure to audiences all her life. That part of the speech was easy. One could be warm, enthusiastic and utterly sincere. The cabinet minister was outside my orbit. I'd never met him and was obliged to do a great deal of research. Obviously, I should have arranged to have a chat with him. But no. Politicians are easy meat and my speech reflected that opinion. The audience enjoyed themselves (so did I) and laughed and laughed. Then, during a wait for a laugh to die, I caught sight of the cabinet minister's face. It was ashen with misery. Too late, I changed tack, made a few conciliatory remarks and sat down quickly to vociferous applause. Then the cabinet minister rose to reply. He said, glumly:

'I can't follow that.'

He went on for a while but he was not a happy man.

The lesson here is clear. One's job in proposing a toast is to show why everyone there is honoured by the presence of the guest; to build him up, to make his the speech of the evening. My vanity had cut the ground from under his feet. For weeks afterwards, people slapped my back and congratulated me. If only they knew – every compliment was a stabwound. Bell learnt: If you have a guest of honour – honour him and stay where you probably belong – at least two rungs down. It's his evening not yours. Give it to him, generously, with both hands and your heart, mind and voice.

Another lesson learnt the hard way was that, if one is going abroad, one should take the trouble to find out whether they have customs peculiar to themselves. An advantage of belonging to a large organization is that there is always someone to ask. You can use the accumulated experience of others. An individual must make the effort himself. There are 101 ways of offending in foreign parts without meaning to. George Bernard Shaw declared that Britain and America were two great nations separated by the same language. He was right. A Britisher using a sentence such as 'He was my fag at Eton' would raise eyebrows in the States where the word 'fag' has homosexual connotations. To say that a girl has a lay mind doesn't just mean that she isn't technical. Neither do you suggest that to correct mistakes she should use a rubber. In

Abu Dhabi a friend described at least ten ways to irritate an Arab, without realizing it. Close neighbours like the Swedes can provide an example. If you are invited to a dinner party – even a small one in somebody's home – and you are placed on the right of the hostess, you are expected at some point to rise to your feet and make a gracious, formal speech. In England we'd look a little sideways at anybody doing that; but our Swedish friends expect it and would regard you as impolite if you failed to rise. It's a delightful custom and should be encouraged.

So if you are likely to speak abroad make a few enquiries first. It will prevent possible embarrassment. Somebody should write a book about the subject. I'll buy it at once.

I would like you to know about a supreme example of a speaker with his thoughts entirely on the interests of his audience. Everyone, kids, even grandfathers called him 'Old Reggie'. Old Reggie was a founder member of our cricket club. He had played at minor county level and taught most of the club members how to play the game. As he grew older he played less; then he served as umpire; at seventy, he became the scorer and we gave him the first in a series of dinners in his honour, followed by dancing. Every five years, Old Reggie spoke at one of his dinners and now that he had become our grand old man at the age of ninety we looked forward to another of his heart-warming speeches. He occupied a room in the hotel where the function was being held and, usually, he sat at dinner with us. But this evening Old Reggie told us he was very tired and would just come down for the speeches. His grandson stayed in the room with him and it became obvious that Old Reggie was in no condition to move, let alone to make an after dinner speech.

'I'll go and tell them that you're too ill to come down' said the grandson.

'Before you do that' murmured Old Reggie, 'Have you got that recording we made at rehearsal?'

'Yes, it's here.'

'Say I'm sorry I can't join in. But I can't let them down. Arrange to have the speech broadcast to them.'

Later, when Old Reggie's voice put across a marvellous talk, many people wept openly. Old Reggie listened to the end of his speech. Then he asked his grandson to come closer and whispered:

'I'm off. Let them enjoy the dancing. Don't tell them until tomorrow.'

Then he smiled, closed his eyes and died.

To return to other occasions. For the past eighty years, the Guild of Professional Toastmasters has recorded each year the name of the worst after dinner speaker endured by its members. Some of the names on this dubious roll of honour are famous: some have earned the toastmasters' thumbs down twice. Neither blandishment nor bribery will make the Guild reveal the culprits until the year 2000. On the other hand, Ivor Spencer, the Guild's president and I discussed which speakers had given us most pleasure – he from his recollection of tens of thousands of speeches and I from my own experience. The list excludes, of course, more excellent speakers than it contains, but these are our choices, in alphabetical order:

Tony Ball
Frank Bough
Graham Dowson
Rachael Heyhoe Flint MBE
Clement Freud MP
Gilbert Grey QC
Lord Mancroft KBE TD
His Honour Judge Sir James Miskin QC DL
Ron Moody
The Baroness Phillips JP
The Viscount Tonypandy
Peter Ustinov CBE

They all have one thing in common – they brought us joy.

They are not only superb speakers but also generous and good fun. Here are some words of advice from them.

Lord Mancroft:
'Some people think that speaking, like sex, ought to come to us all naturally. Maybe it should; but in both cases it's just as well to learn a few tricks.'

Rachael Heyhoe Flint:
'Always prepare even if you think you might not be called upon to speak.

Cut down on the alcohol – an excess certainly does loosen the tongue but it also loosens the brain, making concentration difficult.

Never be over-confident inwardly – but look confident outwardly.'

'Amen' she adds.

Viscount Tonypandy:
'Make sure you know your subject well; leave nothing to chance and then you can leave everything to chance. Do your homework thoroughly. Hard work is still the secret of success. If you know your subject it will come over easily and naturally.

Secondly, do not be afraid to rehearse it at home, speaking it out loud so that you get the sound of the words.

Thirdly, when the time comes for you to address your audience make sure that you direct your speech to the person sitting at the back of the hall. If he can hear you, you may fairly assume that people in between may also do so.

My last brief piece of advice is this: never, if you can avoid it, insult an audience by standing up to speak without adequate preparation. This is unfair both to yourself and those who have to listen to you.'

Ron Moody:
'Words of advice can't be easy because public speaking is such a personal matter. It ranges from the string-of-jokes or one-line-gags speech (which is really a stand-up comedy act) to the long-winded monologue where the public bore indulges in "the exuberance of his own verbosity". I don't admire either. The following words of advice are entirely on my own approach and it works – for me.

* Compose your speech with brevity and humour – respecting the occasion.
# Print it out clearly. Then read it, *exactly as written* with conviction. No dithering to find words. Just sell it!
* This is the tricky bit
# This is the easy bit.'

Baronesss Phillips:
'Be yourself. Know your subject. Talk – don't read. Humour must be related to the topic. Avoid phrases like "I shall have more to say about this later." "Finally" means I am ending this speech *now*.'

Peter Ustinov:
'As to advice to would-be orators, I would say that, in order to take them by surprise – and surprise is an essential ingredient in good speaking, as it is in military strategy and in love – it is imperative to take risks, by taking yourself by surprise. Don't rehearse too meticulously. Don't learn things by heart – and certainly not other people's poetry. "I think it was Kipling who once said . . ." and so on. He probably didn't, and if he did, he shouldn't have. The main thing is to have a point of view, and to release your imagination in the parkland of your subject, like a dog. Then as the dog does, rely on instinct. Don't go on too long. If the public is wonderful, stop a little short of total triumph. If they find you boring, go on a little longer than

necessary, just to punish them. Also resist the temptation to laugh at your jokes before reaching the point. The audience may find this inhibiting, to the point of not wishing to join in the laughter, your laughter. There are many rules, but, as usual, they are there only to be broken.'

Tony Ball:
'Prepare, pretend to be confident, and always flatter the audience. Don't fall over, pick your nose, or pontificate. Use humour, use notes, and use your hands. Smile, weave stories around the appropriate "characters" present, and exude a friendly sincerity. Be natural, be topical and only drink during toasts. Emphasize in threes, include a brief serious message – and pray.'

There you have it in a nutshell from some of the best after dinner speakers in the world. It would be impertinent of me to add anything except to thank them on your behalf. I do so, most warmly.

Exercises

1 After fifty-two years with your company, a senior manager is retiring. You and your colleagues are giving a lunch for him at a local hotel, plus a farewell present. Prepare a speech for the occasion.
2 Your well-established cricket club has recently formed a women's team. At the dinner to celebrate the occasion, you have been wise enough to get Rachael Heyhoe Flint as your Guest of Honour. Prepare to introduce her.
3 You have been asked to propose the toast to your great-uncle and his wife at their diamond wedding. Plan it.
4 As the leading figure in your local Townswomen's Guild you are proposing the toast at a luncheon in honour of the Baroness Phillips. You have worked with her in the National Association for Maternal and Child Welfare. Prepare.

8 Visual aids

The human voice is only one of the channels through which ideas can flow. Sound, sight, touch, smell, taste all provide means of conveying thoughts to other people. A good speaker gives his audience a chance to use as many of their senses as the occasion permits. With a little ingenuity you can give their ears a rest and switch channels. One obvious way of doing this is to show them the point, to demonstrate it. The term 'visual aids' does not mean only blackboard-chalk-and-talk stuff – or flip charts or films or overhead projectors; solid-physical, three-dimensional objects have much more effect. If it is practicable, show them the actual thing you are talking about. Let them handle it, smell it, taste it. Use your zest, imagination and enthusiasm to create a worthwhile experience for your audience.

If you are selling a motorcar, the best visual aid is a test drive. Once you have your prospect not only hearing about the car, reading about the car, looking at the car but handling the car in action, he is practically sold on it. Visual aids should get as near to this concept of reality as possible. You should bear in mind the following order of effectiveness:

1 Your listeners operating the actual product.

2 A demonstration of the product-in-action.
3 Working models.
4 Stationary models.
5 Physical objects.
6 Moving pictures.
7 Enlarged pictorial displays such as are shown with projectors; e.g. slides, exploded drawings, diagrams, graphs, tables of figures, maps, photographs etc.
8 Flip charts, blackboards, flannel boards, magnetic boards – with all of which ideas can be developed en route.
9 Words – which are almost useless as visual aids.

You will have observed that we have ranged from the real, the physical, to the abstract, words. How many presentations have you endured where the speaker stops at the end of almost every sentence, turns his back on you and writes words that he has just spoken? The so-called visual aid reads, for instance:

Consultation
Sophistry
Forward
Challenge
Finalization

All abstract drivel, weasel words, buzz words, simply a distraction. Sometimes the speaker will have a prepared list, which he is really using as his notes. If you are tempted to use words as visuals, think again. Speech should take care of the words; visual aids show and demonstrate matters that cannot be so vividly expressed or so easily absorbed by listening. Using only words, try to describe a spiral staircase to someone who has never seen such a thing. Or would you show him how to use the one in the next room?

In 1985, Michael Buerk, that brilliant TV presenter,

clamped in our minds, forever, the appalling suffering in Africa. I doubt whether you remember a word he spoke but you will never erase from your conscience those horrifying pictures of starving, pot-bellied children, milk-dry mothers and their stark despair. Mr Buerk's presentation ranks as one of the most effective the world has ever known. It shattered complacency all over the globe. It stimulated Bob Geldof to his superhuman work with Band Aid. Geldof hammered compassion into action – humanity at its best, not psalm-singing – and we rejoice in such men. Follow their lead, let your words supplement the visual.

There is nothing new in using visual aids. Man's reaction to a given stimulus has hardly changed since civilization began. Only the technology is different. The Bible provides dozens of examples. So do other sources. In AD 51 when the Romans defeated Caratacus they could easily have slain him on the spot and told the story on their return home. But how much more glorious to organize a triumphal procession with the subjugated leader of the Britons dragged through the streets of Rome as an exhibit in chains. There was no need to talk of triumph; it was there for all to see. A good visual aid provides instant recognition of the point and makes it memorable. Severed heads on spikes, villains in the stocks and public floggings all discouraged would-be wrong-doers who, although mostly illiterate, got the message.

Having lauded the value of visual aids we must now put them firmly in their place. No amount of visual aids will make a badly structured presentation into a good one. For speakers they are supports not foundations.

By all means ease your audience's labour – and listening can be hard work – by giving their ears a rest and switching the input to their eyes. This implies that you talk less while they are looking; and that is how it should be. Let the picture tell the story. It is not a good visual if you have to give it much oral support. A visual aid is a rival for their attention. Do not compete. Supplement. People cannot concentrate on two sources of information at one time unless they are complementary to each other. Let them work on the idea with you and the visual, steering them in double harness, as it were. Give them time to see the point and to haul it in without distracting chatter. Get rid of the visual as soon as it outlives its usefulness then bring their focus back to yourself.

Cinema and television producers work from a different point of departure. They start with the pictorial and then add comment and dialogue to augment what is seen. Their job is to present a picture show. A speaker's task is to speak and sometimes to augment speech with things seen. On some occasions it is possible to use other senses such as touch and even smell.

Many talks fail because slapdash eager-beavers skip the purpose – people – proposition – power points – and profit stage and rush straight to the decorations – pasting up the wallpaper without first making sure that the house has foundations and drains that work. Note any visual ideas that occur to you during stage one – the brainstorming stage, but pay no particular attention to them at this time. Leave them noted but undeveloped until you have thoroughly organized your thinking at stage two. Techniques and discipline work hard for you. Do not treat your friends with contempt. Not until you know what you are doing – and why; only when you have a driving purpose and a structure supporting you should you sort out how to display and deliver the goods.

A man visiting America to make a presentation said to an underling 'I'm too busy to prepare. Write a few transparencies for me and I'll talk round them'. The trip cost thousands of pounds. He came back empty-handed and wondered why!

Visual aids help your listeners. They are not crutches for poor speakers. Cue cards, for instance, should act only as prompters, not as substitutes for intelligent preparation and eye contact. If a man is too lazy or too busy to do a professional speaking job he should not be allowed to waste people's time. Visual aids support the talk. They clarify, simplify, and link with what is known and recognized: but they are adjuncts not the master.

The overhead projector

This gadget has become an instrument of torture. It was originally intended to be used by academics who stood at floor level with enlarged pictures projected high above their

Figure 9

heads on to a raised screen. The speaker could thus face his audience, point out particular features of the illustration and sketch in new data as his lecture proceeded. A splendid idea. But what happens now – it is used in rooms so low that the screen cannot be sited high enough. The projector itself stands on a table at navel level and the speaker usually gets in the way. This contraption has spawned an additional link in the Ascent of Man. We've had the Neanderthal Man, we've had the Cro-Magnon Man. Now we have the original Transparent Man, who believes that wherever he stands we can see through him. He is a fast breeder, spreading rapidly wherever men speak. He looms large before screen and flip chart, blackboard or map. (See Figure 9.)

The overhead projector is here to stay and is too good an instrument to ignore. So we have got to learn to live with it. If you can operate it as was originally intended with the projected picture well overhead, with the speaker at floor level allowed easy access to the box and free movement – good. If you are obliged to present talks in an office or a training room not properly designed for the job, you have some rehearsing and experimental work to do. Get yourself a stand-in. Sit in various parts of the room. Check the sight lines. Keep in mind that there will be other bodies to cope with and have your friend perform parts of your talk. You will soon spot the dangers. Can you move the screen to a better position? Can you move the box to a better position? If your rectangular picture looks like a lozenge or other odd shapes try various focuses: tip the screen forward at the top. Is it feasible for you to obtain a curved screen placed in a corner of the working area? Can you rearrange the seating? One method is to work almost at right angles to your audience with the box on one side. (See Figure 10.)

This arrangement also leaves you a clear working area to use when you switch off the projector – no box in the way.

Another useful variation when dealing with a comparatively small audience is to have them seated so that they form

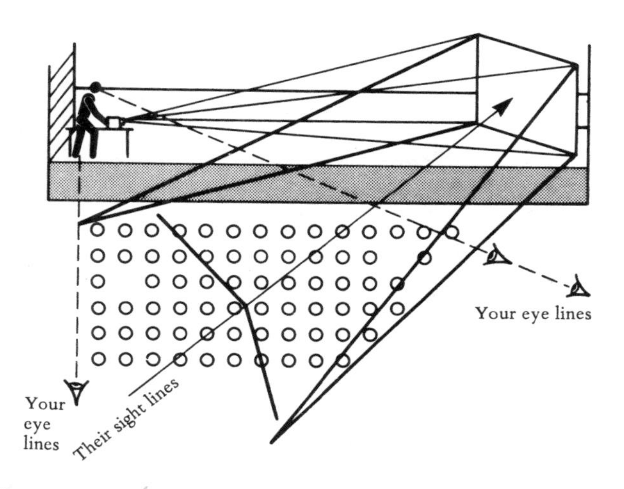

Figure 10

two sides of a triangle or horseshoe with the screen completing the triangle. You operate from the box placed at the apex – facing the screen. This arrangement means that you lose their eyes and it is only recommended for a distinct part or parts of your presentation. Allow ample space for your movements to and from the working area. (See Figure 11.)

Experiment with other settings to suit the room, the clarity of your projections and the comfort of your audience.

The overhead projector will not cease to be a nuisance all by itself. It can be a blessing, but like all blessings has to be deserved. You've got to work on it with your audience fully in your mind. Don't trust to luck on the day. Make your own luck. Tame the brute. Know well where the off switch is situated. Get rid of the glare and noisy hum. Unless you are using a rapid flow of transparencies, switch off.

Be thrifty, almost mean about how much information you display on each transparency. 'Accentuate the positive;

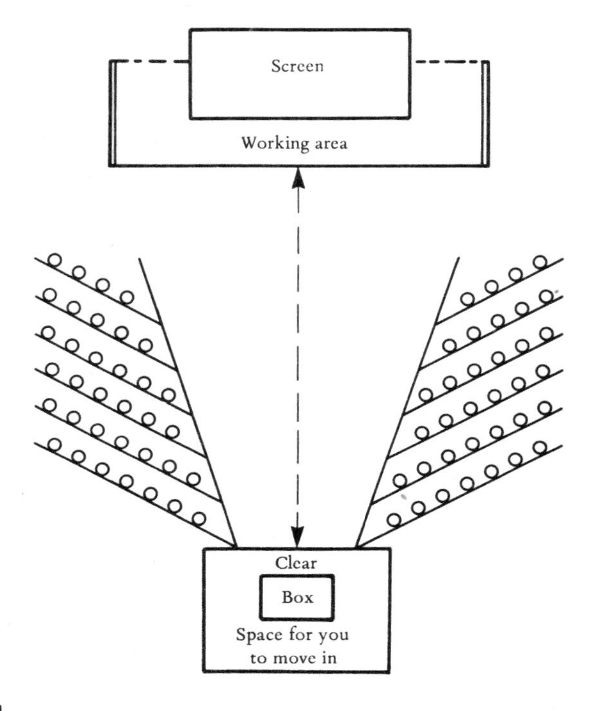

Figure 11

eliminate the negative' says the old song. If you are tempted to tear out pages of a typed report and reproduce them with extraneous material confusing the listeners you can hardly expect them to concentrate on your point. There is so much else to read, including thumbprints and greasy, grey splodges. Create fresh, stripped-to-the-point visuals with the fact in mind that your listeners are not sitting quietly at home reading a report at their own pace. They must keep up with yours. Again, unlike readers, they cannot refer back or re-read the tricky bits. If they do not grasp the point in one go, it's lost, maybe forever. Plan the layout, the lettering, colours etc. on paper before committing them to the transparencies. Some clever people can write the whole of the Lord's Prayer on a pinhead. Let them have their fun, but don't inflict such eyestraining miniatures on your audience. Make everything bold so that the point strikes them at once. Use clear, concise labels. Watch margins – be generous. It is a simple matter to make and to work with a frame within which all the material fits comfortably. A discreet layer of tape on two corners, marked 'top' will ensure that you need not worry about placing things upside down or back to front. Overhead projections pall after the first three or four. Ruthlessly weed out every one of them not absolutely vital – or you will suffer a diminishing return, probably by the time you reach something important.

Have your props organized and ready to hand. Whilst you are fiddling about searching for transparencies you lose contact unless you make a determined effort to stay with your audience.

One way to avoid such fumbling is to have a series of transparencies on a roller; you simply turn the handle to your next illustration.

Overlays can be effective. As the name implies, one transparency is laid on another to introduce more information. Fasten them on one side, like a small booklet, so that they fall into the right position as you use each one. Colour variations can be used for additional effect and to keep the merging concepts clear.

The peek-a-boo trick – this is where you have a list of words covered up and you expose them one at a time – like a striptease girl taking off her wraps. She occasionally slips and uncovers more than she intended at this moment, coyly giggling at her error. If you use the peek-a-boo, keep it under control. Don't take too long over the first two or three garments, as it were, or your audience will begin to estimate how many more they have to wait for and for how long, and grow impatient. You are not in the tease business. They want you to come to the point.

The flip chart

The flip chart provides the presenter with a most useful aid. It has a few drawbacks. It is not of much use in a large auditorium, but with a limited number of listeners, say up to fifty, flip charts help a talk to flow and are easy to use. But, and this is a big but, Transparent Man often takes over. He tends to write words and draw pictures and, while you are wondering whether his face is less unattractive than his backside, he chats to his artwork, lovingly admiring it as if he'd just painted a Rembrandt. You, of course, are fully aware that your diagram will not show through your body like an x-ray photograph. You'll want to keep clear. You know what is on the chart, and you'll think it idiotic to gawp at it and block the view of those you wish to share the information. So, first of all, you must place the charts and their stand in the most advantageous position – usually centre stage – with enough room all round so that you can move freely either side of it. Should you be using two stands, position one on each side of you with adequate space for you to work in. You check sight lines of course. Assuming that you are right-handed, the basic position for your body is slightly behind and to the right of the stand. Try this: grip the edge of the chart with your left hand and move away, right, to an easy arm's length clear of the chart and about a foot back. Think of your gripping hand as a hinge. Draw what you have to draw with your right hand. This of course takes your body across the chart. Then, using the hinge, swing your whole body back to the basic position and show what you have drawn to the people most awkwardly placed – those on your extreme right. Catch their eyes. If they can see your chart so can everybody else. In general make a practice of working much of the time deliberately to the people on your right. It will help you to keep clear. This technique is particularly important if you are obliged to use a board fixed to the back wall. Start your illustrations on your far left and work towards the right. In that way you will not mask what you have drawn earlier in your exposition, should you still need it.

The peek-a-boo can be particularly irritating on a flip chart. The method is to fold up the bottom edge of the chart to hide all except one item. Then, by messing about with clips or sticky tape, adjusting the paper to reveal the next item. Far better to use more than one stand, e.g. your first point being established, say a general map of the area, use a second chart to show a topographical detail and how it relates to the whole. If you have only one stand use two charts, the first showing item one, the second repeating item one plus item two. Place a clear sheet of paper between each drawing otherwise the next one tends to show through and distract. Although much of your flip chart work will seem to be spontaneous you must plan beforehand on sheets of A4 paper all that you intend to show. A4 has about the same proportions as a sheet of flip chart paper, roughly 3 × 2.

Then sketch in on your flip charts very lightly in pencil or by making subtle indentations, guide lines which you can follow when using your felt pen. Lead pencil can also be used on a blackboard. Those of us with little artistic ability can thus draw perfect circles, rectangles and perspectives with the best of them. To cut down drawing time, some of your charts could be fully prepared in advance, or outlined for later development. You then only need to expose them at the appropriate time. Cover your drawing with a blank sheet as soon as it is done with. If you intend to return to it later, arrange to find it easily. A small fold or a tab on the corner of the paper with a number or another identifying symbol saves much groping.

Some speakers use their charts as a running summing-up by fixing them, en passant, in a suitable place with thumbtacks or putty; but this can be messy, unless neatly done, and a misspelt word becomes a magnet for the duration. Or did you check your spelling? 'Magnet' takes us on to one of the most useful visual aids.

The magnetic board

This is a large sheet of steel, securely based, on which you fasten charts, maps, etc. with strips or coin-size magnets. You will immediately see the possibilities of building up, with cardboard cut-outs, jigsaw fashion, the layout of, say, an engine or a factory. No chalk, no pens – simply place your pieces and fix them with a magnet. You can introduce a variety of colours in such exhibits as a simple pie chart or the growth of an empire. Sometimes the pieces themselves are magnetic and you can show how component parts slot in with each other.

Magnetic string can link one part of a flow chart to another. Variations in simple circuits can be explained and you can slide pieces about to show movement in what you are describing. Titles, labels and significant figures can be emphasized by merely attaching them – no time wasted while you write them.

The magnetic board demands no dimming of the lights; no bulbs burn out. There are no electrical contacts, no switches to worry about. But do not use a magnetic board on an easel. If a peg should slip, the heavy steel could separate you from your toes or cause some other damage. Unfortunately steel boards are not easily portable. There is an apparatus on the market which provides a combination of flip charts, white board, magnetic board and several other advantages. This piece of equipment is mounted on rollers and can easily be moved to suit the needs of your audience. If you are a teacher with a permanent conference room you should immediately present a case to obtain this asset.

But the money is, perhaps, not available, so you must settle for the magnetic board's first cousin – the flannel board.

The flannel board

This is a rigid board covered with flannel or felt or similar material. An old blanket will serve. Using lightweight cardboard, you create your diagrams and other pieces and fix a strip of sandpaper or flock on the back of each one. Press the backs to the flannel – and press firmly – and there you are. You will not be able to move your pieces so easily on the flannel board as with the magnetic board. A flannel board could be a do-it-yourself job.

Another useful do-it-yourself job is a stand for intimate desktop presentations. Make a base, either solid or just a frame, 2½ft. × 1ft., and hinge it . . . oh, let's make it visual, shall we? (See Figure 12.)

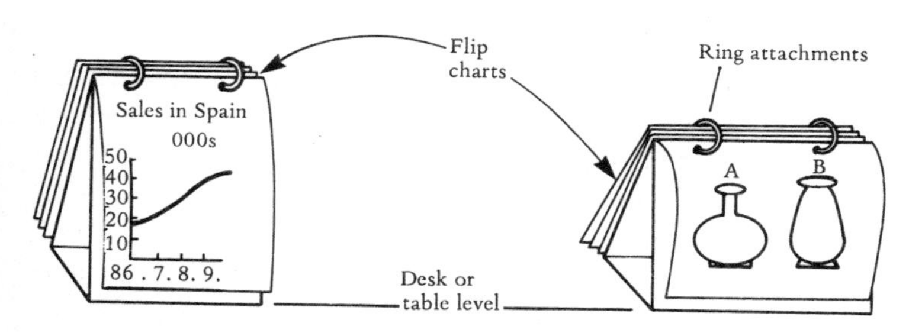

Figure 12

You know exactly what each chart shows; you have identification on the back of the chart which follows. So you can stand behind them or on one side facing your listeners, turning each page as you proceed. This apparatus could be collapsible for easy transportation.

Slides

Our great-grandfathers used a contraption called the magic lantern. We use a slide projector, which is much the same thing. Both instruments display still pictures, but great-grandpa did not have the advantages of superior colour photography, delicate focusing, quick changeover from one slide to another, remote control, reverse control, hand-held control, and well-trained specialists who, so long as we treat them kindly and know what we want, provide splendid slides for us. There is no excuse nowadays for anything less than perfect slides and a perfect presentation of them.

Slides are one of the most versatile and effective of all aids. They can bring item, chart or panorama to the audience. They are easily stored, durable, portable. Like all good visual aids slides should:

1. Illustrate only one point at a time.
2. Show the object under discussion prominently.
3. Show nothing irrelevant.
4. Have plain backgrounds, e.g. the lizard is what we should be studying, not the stone tower on which it perches. (Is that Majorca or Cyprus? I've seen that tower somewhere before!)
5. And slides should *make the point.*

Reasonably well cared for, slides will serve you for years to come. If you are offered stock slides from the library, refuse to accept them unless they are exactly what is required. Don't show a whole depot with fifteen dustcarts in order to demonstrate how the machine that minces the garbage works. I saw this one only last week. The picture sticks in the mind of trios of grinning dustmen in laundry-fresh overalls proudly posing before their gleaming new vehicles. The speaker bleated that this was the only slide he could get. Be firm, insistent. Your slides are going to last for a long time. Get the best. Why should you need to apologize because 'this slide doesn't exactly show what I mean very well'.

Murphy's Law: 'If a thing can go wrong it will go wrong' might have been inspired by the slide presentation. You must take every precaution to circumvent Murphy. 'That'll do' is his cue to prove you wrong.

You will recall that the talk is primary, the illustrations

secondary. Having got your talk structured in a thoroughly professional manner, go to the expert slide-maker. You of course know what you want but you will pick his brain and, at least, listen to his advice. Motivate him to share in your success. If you happen to be skilful enough to make your own slides, that's fine. But you won't mind if we pause here to give the less skilful some basic information to prepare him for his meeting with the slide-maker.

What goes on to the slide is your responsibility. Draw up a set of suggested graphs, photographs, line diagrams, etc; collect objects such as solid components that you intend to use for your slides. The professional slide-maker will know a good deal about colouring, optics and matters such as the ratio of viewing distance to the height of the letters. He will be well aware of the recommendations of the British Standards Institution. But he will not thank you if you present him with a fait accompli; so discuss your slides with him before you take the photographs. Keep your drawings open to change. For example, if you were seeing the following information for the first time, which of these presentations of the data would you prefer – Figure 13(a) or (b) or (c) or (d)?

Figure 13(a)

The sales for May to October were 20 of type 1, 32 of type 2, 38 of type 3; for June, 28 of type 1, 30 of type 2, 36 of type 3; for July, 40 of type 1, 30 of type 2, 28 of type 3; for August, 26 of type 1, 18 of type 2, 28 of type 3; for September, 26 of type 1, 18 of type 2, 30 of type 3, and for October, 44 of type 1, 20 of type 2 and 28 of type 3.

Figure 13(b)

Sales figures for May to October

	Type 1	Type 2	Type 3
May	20	32	38
June	28	30	36
July	40	30	28
August	26	18	28
September	26	18	30
October	44	20	28

Figure 13(c)

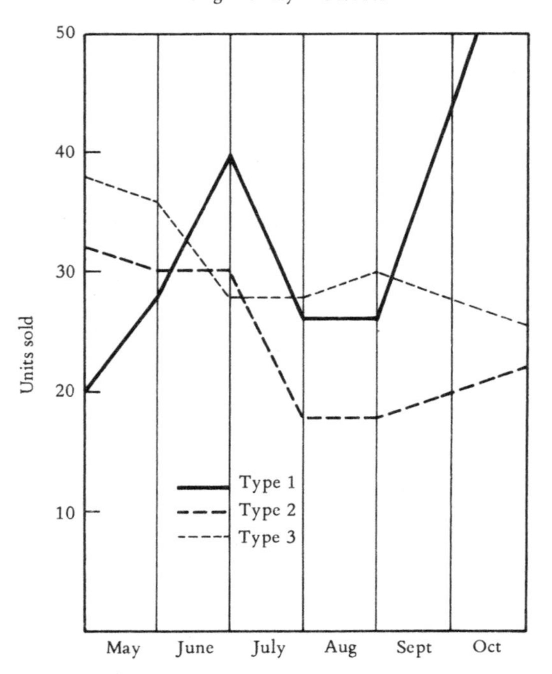

You would probably use different colours with (c) and (d) to add emphasis; or perhaps make the bar chart horizontal. There is a choice. Explain to him exactly what

Figure 13(d)

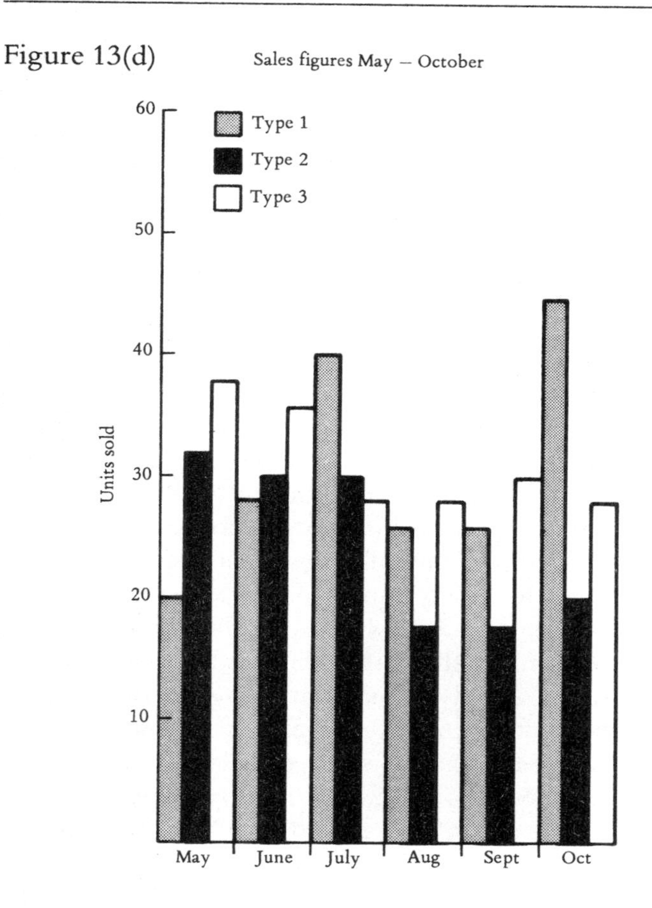

you wish your audience to gain from each slide (he might even be able to help you with the weeding).

When you receive the finished slides, number them with small stick-on, but not permanent, labels. You might want to change the numbers later. The traditional position for such labels is on the bottom left-hand corner when hand-held for viewing. Wherever you position the labels, be consistent – you might have to find them in the dark. Also it is easier to sort slides if you know exactly where the numbers are.

In some establishments the machine itself is situated at the back of the hall and is operated by a projectionist. More modern halls are equipped so that the speaker has direct control from a hand-held unit or a console. This obviates the need for cueing signals for 'next slide', 'house lights', 'curtains drawn' and so on.

The TV weathermen provide excellent examples – map and chart changes, isobars and fronts moving, clouds crossing, temperature, wind strength and direction. Watch how unobtrusively they handle the control button. How expertly they maintain eye contact and how good the graphics are. They make it all look so simple and easy; but such precision demands thought, rehearsal, discipline and keeping ever in their minds millions of viewers.

If you employ the services of a projectionist, probably the local man in charge of the hall, you will already have made a friend of him. He already knows that he is an important part of your presentation. Treat him as your partner. Probably he has worked more slide presentations than you ever will. He may be the one giving you the following advice.

Load the slides into the magazine in his presence and explain, if necessary, why you have blanks in the series, why some slides are repeated, duplicated. The blanks, of course, provide a blank screen and save him the trouble of switching the machine off when no picture is needed. The duplicates save him the trouble of going back to search for the slide, used five minutes ago, to which you are again referring. Rehearse all signals for, for instance, switching on and off the house lights; rehearse cues for a change of slide. These cues must be scripted or made completely clear in some other agreed way. Check that the control switch has clear indicators for forward and reverse. Check that spares are available and their precise whereabouts. What happens if a fuse blows or a lamp fails? What will you do if there is a power cut? Have you a contingency working of your presentation and reserve props to see you through?

With a well-structured talk you should be able to cope.

Rehearse. Rehearse. Rehearse, especially the props.

If you make a verbal slip you can easily put that right, but a wayward prop cannot redeem itself.

Here are some examples of speakers who managed when the apparatus went awry or the slides were mislaid.

A mountaineer described an overhang at umpteen thousand feet and how it had to be mastered. He took several sheets of flip chart paper, crumpled and fastened them into the shape of a snow-covered mountain (see Figure 14). There was the mountain top on the table. He manipulated part of his mountain to illustrate an overhang and explained that the problem was to get from A to B with no visible means of support and a drop of 1400 feet. He demonstrated by fixing spikes into a plank at the back of the stage and climbed to the ceiling. Then he took us with him in our imagination, step by perilous step, high above our heads, the whole length of the hall. We cheered when he achieved his goal at B. The mountaineer never used a slide again for that part of his talk.

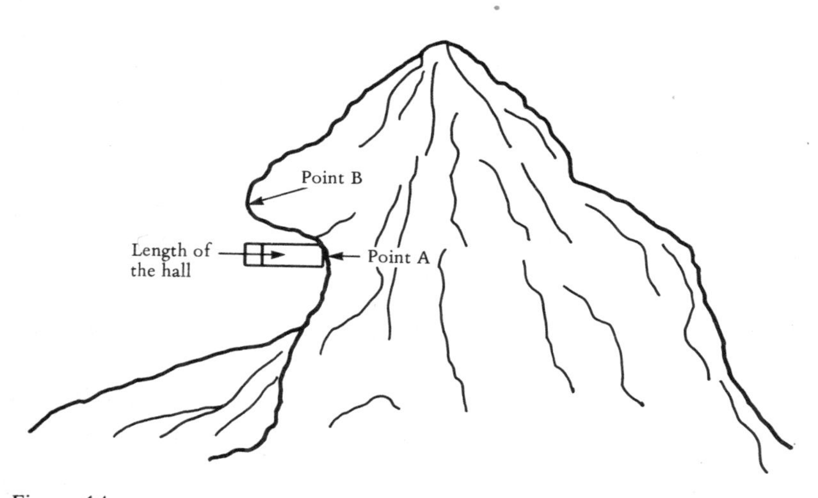

Figure 14

A diver used the opposite approach. As we dropped into the water with him and sank, the ceiling became the surface of the water and the lights gradually dimmed until we were in the dark except for his torch. A fire extinguisher, strapped to his back, became his breathing apparatus. We took part in an exciting underwater event. Who wants just talk?

A horsewoman, illustrating the height and length of a jump by a steeplechaser, simply turned the table on its edge, added a box or two and – I can see her now – skipped from one side of the stage, took us over the jump with a sweeping wave of her hand and we landed at the other side an incredible distance away from the take-off point. Now, any rider who falls off – even when I've backed his horse – has my sympathy and admiration. I've experienced that jump and what he is up against.

An engineer had invented a valve which speeded up the delivery of high octane spirit into aircraft – a most important saving of time during which danger lurks. He wished to make the point that the supply came from vast tanks, and he'd lost his notes with all the cubic figures, etc. Few of us would have grasped them anyway. But when he explained that if we took the whole lecture theatre and put another one on top of it and that that was the amount of high octane spirit that had to be shifted at speed, we understood perfectly.

Moving pictures

Cinema attendances have declined since the advent of television. Nowadays only a superb or well-hyped motion picture can persuade people to stir from their homes when they have much the same entertainment on tap in their living rooms. It is not unknown for viewers to watch for a few minutes then to lapse into a gentle snooze, so commonplace has the moving picture become. There are several risks to be considered if you intend to make a film show part of your presentation. In a dim or darkened room heads tend to nod, eyes to close, and reverberating sounds of slumber compete with the dialogue. And you have no control; you yielded that as soon as the film took over. With a cassette you can stop, back-track, and start again, interpolate, develop what is shown and move on to the next point. With a film you are out for the duration. Analyses of what audiences have understood and remembered often reveal that they remember the famous funny man and how he made them laugh but not the point under consideration.

I am not denigrating films, far from it. Having spent many years in the industry, I know the value of accomplished film-makers and their products.

At this stage, my thoughts must stay with you as a speaker using films as an aid. All forms of communication are a struggle for other people's attention. As has been noted before, visual aids compete with you unless you use them properly. Use them – don't let them obliterate you.

It is common to see a less than dedicated trainer switch on the film, note that it runs for eighteen minutes, then slope off to put his feet up somewhere. Almost invariably such people do not command their subject fully and are using the film to fill the gaping holes in their knowledge. No good manager delegates to the extent that he doesn't even know what his subordinate contributes.

So if you intend to use a film, take the trouble to visit the suppliers and examine everything appropriate they have to offer. Do not merely buy a title, whatever the blurb says. Having bought or hired your film, get to know it frame by frame. Run it many times. Often, it could inspire you to re-cast and improve the whole of your presentation. When you know exactly what you want your audience to take in, tell them in advance what to look for. Alternatively, run it once without comment; discuss the important elements; remind them what you wish them to remember. Then run it again. But stay with it so that you remain part of its message. There are, of course, many occasions when this procedure is not feasible: but you must never underestimate the power of a good film. Contrive to keep it on your side.

Particularly at training sessions, a film skilfully used can add stature to the trainer and maintain his authority – so long as he does not concede it.

Physical objects

You know what a cigarette looks like so I would only need the word to put one into your thoughts. But supposing I said: 'universal joint' (no, sir, not a doped cigarette passed from mouth to mouth among a group of junkies). Would you instantly know what a universal joint looks like? Perhaps so, perhaps not. I could describe it to you in fifty words. Or would you rather see one and discover how it works in a practical demonstration?

Unless you are showing something colossal, physical objects cannot be used effectively with a large audience. Of course you can show them, say, a crankshaft and then project an enlarged picture of it on to a screen.

An engineer used this technique most effectively. He specialized in knitting machines and wished to discuss with fellow specialists six different needles, their various uses and values. The audience consisted of only twenty-five people. When we arrived at the conference room, we found on our desks six needles, various yarns and sample weaves lying on a piece of baize. Each item was labelled for identification. Of course we picked them up and fiddled about with them. The speaker encouraged us to do so, and then to put them on the baize in numerical order and to leave them there.

He had exhausted our temptation to fiddle – rather like a parson friend of mine who, in the winter, always prefaced his sermon by telling the congregation to cough, sneeze, blow their noses, and get it out of their systems. When the subsequent jolly storm of nasal and bronchial clearances subsided, he began. Hardly a sniff stirred the air for the next eight minutes (he was a sensible preacher and kept it short).

To return to our knitting. We followed the projected pictures, we handled the needles and the latches and did a little meshing, all under his control. This presentation happened at least ten years ago, but though I am not an engineer, those six needles and their uses are still clear in my mind.

Allowing an audience to handle samples etc. is never an easy matter, especially if they have to pass them round to each other. The basic technique here is that you first tell them precisely what to look for and, while the object is circulating, bring in nothing new. With a small group, circulate yourself, repeat the detail to be observed and keep the object firmly in your hand thus controlling the speed of the circulation. If you have a large audience, post helpers at the ends of the rows and provide plenty of samples – plenty, preferably one for each member of the audience, especially if the object is an agreeable takeaway. But in general such proceedings can break up even a first class talk and are better avoided.

You can show an audience too much. A splendid model of a railway engine may well have the cognoscenti criticizing the livery when you wish to discuss the flanges on the wheels. Would you choose a gorgeous looking actress as an aid to a lecture on how the inner structure of the body works? If you did, the mean sensual males in your audience would contemplate the curve of her breast rather than how the hip bone connects to the thigh bone; and the ladies would wonder how she obtained such uplift.

If I may refer back to the question 'What do I do with my hands?', many speakers find comfort at the start of a presentation from using a hand-held prop to make the first point. This device is a lame substitute for being more interested in them than yourself, but better a crutch than disaster. So – if you need to – use this idea. Also, a few props suitably deployed can provide you with reasons for natural movement to new positions during your talk. An audience can only focus on a fixed point for a limited period. Give them a new angle from time to time. One of the worst drawbacks in reading a paper from a lectern is that, out there, there are several hundred cricks in several hundred necks. Give them relief. Move.

Demonstrations of the product in action are not always possible e.g. Epsom salts at work on a patient. So we create a model to show the effect. In recounting the following example I am, in a way, sublimating my disgust in having been part of it. It happened a long time ago, in fact it was only my second production of a commercial show. I've changed all the names. We'll call the product Crappo. Crappo was a leading brand of detergent and the company, to celeberate its centenary, was proudly presenting the public with a great new product called New Crimson Crappo – It's New! It's Crimson! It's Crappo!

My job was to send 600 of their salesmen away from the presentation all shiny-eyed and glorying in the new product. The presentation took the form of a hundred years of old songs and dances culminating in:

NOW! AT LAST! THE ULTIMATE! AND A DITTY CALLED 'IT'S NEW. IT'S CRIMSON. IT'S CRAPPO!'

The rehearsals in London went well and the singers and dancers arrived on site ready to go.

I had been inexperienced enough to leave parts of the script uncompleted. I wanted to talk to the laboratory people and get the facts correct for the scientific bit – you know, where the men in white coats tell us: 'Scientists say . . .' with dollops of jargon, all very impressive. 'What', I asked the Director of Research, 'were the facts substantiating claims that this new stuff disposes of grease more quickly, was kinder to ladies' hands and so on?' I had my notebook at the ready but he was looking at me with a mixture of horror, disbelief and pity.

'You must be joking, Bell,' he said. 'It's exactly the same as the old stuff except we've got glossy new packaging and we've added a bit of dye. Didn't you know?'

'So it's phoney. Do your salesmen know?'

'Of course not.'

'What about the public?'

'They'll be queuing up for it. You should see the advertising. Subtle. Not a lie in it. Marvellous. Any shop that hasn't got plenty in stock will feel a draught when we launch.'

'But it's phoney.'

'There's no need to be rude.'

I exploded. In a few hundred ill-chosen words I traced his wrong-side-of-the-blanket ancestry and that of all concerned with Crappo. The show will not go on . . .

'You realize,' he purred, 'that there will be no pay for your cast and . . .'

Let us draw a veil over the fact that the show must and eventually did go on; I've been ashamed of this ever since. Now the problem was how to use my ideas demonstrating that grease succumbed to New Crimson Crappo better than to the old product. I'd had two huge plastic containers made, tubular and ten feet high by three feet in diameter, both filled with grease. My plan had been that, at each, a man in a white coat would mount a ladder; the first would pour in the old product and the grease would reduce by about a quarter. Then the second white-coat would pour in the New Crimson Crappo and hey presto! The grease would almost entirely disappear. You will have guessed the answer. Container one remained full of grease; container two was filled with a look-alike substitute.

The show was a great success, the girls and the old songs, lots of fun and nostalgia. I sat out front between the Sales Director and the Managing Director. The men in the white coats did their stuff. There was thunderous applause. The Sales Director turned to me and said 'By God, Bell, this new stuff is marvellous, isn't it?' and he meant it.! Although he was party to the plot he was as completely taken in as the applauding salesmen.

It was later reported that they sold two and a quarter million extra packets during the first month.

I donated my fee to the Actors' Benevolent Fund. The industry's watchdogs, Actors' Equity, and new laws now protect artistes and the public from such shenanigans. Not before time.

As a friendly gesture to me, please forget the story but remember the point. A model often highlights a fact more clearly than the real thing.

Now, let us come to your most important visual aid – you.

The advice is sometimes given that a would-be speaker should practise gestures while looking in a mirror. I am dead against this sort of thing because it tends to focus the speaker on himself, and the gestures are likely to be unnatural, anyway. But you have need to consider seriously that all through your talk you are in view and what the audience sees in you is important. Many of us were absent when the good looks were being handed out so we have to make the best of what we have. If you happen to be an outstandingly beautiful woman or an exceptionally handsome man the audience should be much more aware of the fact than you, apparently, are. Let us admire you but don't join in the chorus. Blatant self-approval always strikes a sour note. There may be occasions where the recommendation 'If you've got it – flaunt it!' makes sense; but speaking is not one of them.

Everything about you sends out signals: that old Etonian tie, the Savile Row suit, a lady's too-revealing slit skirt, overdone make-up, dirty shoes or bright yellow patent ones – with tweeds; earrings on a man, long hair, short back and sides, a pleasing grin or a false bonhomie. Matters of this sort strike us before you have even said a word; and the cumulative effect stays with us throughout your talk.

A speaker must develop a sense of the occasion and dress for it. Men have less trouble than women. If the rig called for is tails, dinner jacket or sober suits they have no problem. Women have to give the subject much more thought. The essential factors which shape your decision about dress must be the occasion and your attitude to the people attending it. You can dress up too much or, what is worse, condescend by dressing down. If HRH The Princess of Wales were asked to speak to an audience composed of ordinary working people would she daub grime on her face and hands and appear in soiled workaday clothes to indicate that she was one of them? Of course not. Her instinctive good manners would tell her that they would take offence at such a deplorable masquerade.

People dislike the phoney. There are army officers who will walk into the Sergeants' Mess and use obscene language to show that they can be one of the boys and can 'come down to our level'. Subordinates despise such louts. Their attitude is patronizing and nauseating.

In short, whether the occasion is the Lord Mayor's banquet or a lecture, the speaker must make us *comfortable* with the way in which he presents himself. You are your own most important visual aid. It's worth some thought.

9 The big show

'Britain in further slide against economic rivals' (*Times* headline).

According to the annual survey made by the European Management Forum Foundation only three leading European economies – those of France, Italy and Spain – are doing worse.

' "Coventry has lost more than 60,000 manufacturing jobs in ten years," say council economists. Their findings in the latest edition of the city council's economic monitor show that manufacturing jobs fell from 119,634 to just 57,700 in ten years – a drop of more than half' (*Coventry Evening Telegraph*).

Has this got anything to do with speaking? You may well ask.

I was called to the telephone one evening at my home. The man at the other end could be described as an important figure in the business world. He apologized for bothering me at home but the matter was urgent, he said. He needed help. He had just taken over as Managing Director of a huge company; but I could not honestly congratulate him because the company was known to be on the skids – going downhill at speed and out of control. He himself described it as a disaster area. His immediate problem was that the company, competing for a contract, had booked the most expensive conference hall in London. Two hundred and forty-eight people, mostly from abroad, including royalty, government ministers, technical advisers and other VIPs, plus wives, were being accommodated at Claridges, the Connaught, Grosvenor House and other such pricey lodgings – and all expenses paid so that they could attend the company's presentation of its proposal.

'Sounds all right. What's the trouble?'

'It's the chap who is making the presentation. I asked to see a run-through. It's appalling, dreadful, absolutely desperate. Can you come down and sort it out for us?'

'We've got a speaking workshop next week', I said. 'Let's have him for a few days to give him the basics of speaking and then we can work with him on this particular presentation.'

'There's no time for that. The presentation is on Thursday.'

This was Tuesday evening.

I suggested that, since he himself was a first class speaker, thoroughly trained, that he should take over and do it personally.

'You don't know this chap. He's obstinate as a mule; says that as the Financial Director he's the only one who knows the figures and no one else is going to be allowed to touch it – etc., etc.'

It was a forlorn hope, but we arranged that I should be at their works at eight o'clock the following morning. The atmosphere, to put it mildly, was decidedly unfriendly. Mr X made no bones about being furious that I had been called in. He behaved like an enraged bull – perhaps because everybody had been goading him. The picadors had speared him; the banderilleros had thrust in their darts. I felt that he should be left alone in the ring, with me as a sort of matador aiming not for death in the afternoon but for success tomorrow. When we had pushed everybody else out of the room I suggested that perhaps Mr X would like to make his presentation exactly as he intended so that I could grasp the main outline of his case. Reluctantly, he agreed. The time was 08.46.

At 10.04, after one hour and eighteen minutes of non-stop balderdash, he stopped talking. Mr X was not only wooden, but the deathwatch beetle had got into him as well. As an inflicter of pain he made Torquemada look like a novice. His chief weapon was an overhead projector upon which he scurried along fifty-four projections with an average viewing time of four seconds. One transparency contained 3628 digits; another, a three-dimensional statistical graph requiring a degree in economics for comprehension. The only visual aids which remained long enough even to read were his notes from which he recited his speech. When it was tactfully suggested that perhaps we could work together to improve matters he became, well, abusive is not too strong a word. One had to bite back phrases like ‘pompous ass’, ‘spoilt brat’, ‘nut case’, and do one’s best.

On their return, his colleagues and I offered several suggestions but he dug his heels in up to the armpits. Secretly, a working party and I slogged all night on a fresh presentation in the hope that a new day might bring some sense. Could Mr X have a diplomatic illness? Poison was suggested, almost seriously. But Mr X defeated us all. His fellow directors had gone through all this before and shrugged their shoulders. Short of sacking him on the spot, the new MD had no option but to let it go.

At the presentation, twenty minutes was long enough for the Royals and the Sheiks to discover that they had another engagement. They departed with their entourages – not too quietly. The few who, perforce, remained to the end made polite noises and left with little ceremony and some speed.

The contract was worth £184 million, plus maintenance contracts and more to follow. Apart from the cash, the jobs lost ran into thousands.

The sad tail to this episode is that Mr X, who knew how to frame his own contract, was persuaded to retire – with a golden handshake worth more than most engineers earn in a lifetime. Even sadder is the fact that Mr X is not unique among our captains of industry.

The main requirements for a successful business are: enough satisfied customers, with profit for both sides, and repeat orders. It seems to me that British industry suffers from a surfeit of accountants and book-keepers who have taken over from the men who can make things and sell them – men who know about customers and their needs. Customers have become far less important than elegant balance sheets. It is easy enough to make a case for buying a computer and sacking workers. It looks good on paper; but the true result is often disastrous. Who goes when redundancy is in the air – the duds – at all levels? Not on your life! The baby gets thrown out with the bath water and skilled men and women rust in idleness. Cut. Retrench. Cut. It is all so negative.

If we've got a million or two to invest, why not invest it in the positive, in people, and a drive for more business? Then we might need two computers to cope with the extra trade. The customers and the business are there in plenty. Our competitors make this painfully clear – or have you not noticed Japanese cars, American TV and their films swamping the market? Even Scotch whisky is in peril from highly skilled operators selling ersatz. Some companies spend fortunes on advertising, sponsored sport, 'prestige' offices and so on, but only pennies on the development of people within the organization. Training budgets in the UK are a national scandal.

Let's go back to Mr X. At college he received no communications training at all. In the subsequent thirty years, he never took his coat off in, or even visited, the workshops. He came to regard salesmen as vulgar carpet-baggers and research people as a costly nuisance. Customers and products were shadowy, far-distant factors that only became real in the accounts. Why some chairman hadn't taken him by the scruff of the neck and obliged him to join the hurly-burly of trade for a couple of weeks a year passes comprehension. Equally, every other manager and specialist should be lifted from his rut now and then to learn and to appreciate what goes on elsewhere – to understand what money means to an accountant, what customers look like face to face, how the design people set to work, how the unions operate and, above all, to develop his own personal skills to the full – especially how to speak for the company at all times.

If we look at another presentation, perhaps we can see where all this fits in.

The location is a lovely mansion in the country and several hundred potential buyers have been invited to come to the show. The reception – pretty girls and a glass of champagne, personal information folders with our names grandly printed and beaming smiles all round – could not have been bettered. The whole house breathed culture, dignity and gracious living. We were escorted to the theatre, and to our reserved seats. The people who designed and made the scenery really knew their business. The sets rivalled the beauty of the house and the fifty video screens were unobtrusive. A twenty-strong team of technicians and stage managers would bring us music on cue, lights on cue, special effects, filmed inserts. The stage would revolve and colours change at the touch of a switch. Fifteen hundred cues had to be obeyed with split-second timing. From every seat every nuance of the performance would be visible and every sound perfect.

Lights, music – on with the show.

A splendid young lady, thoroughly experienced and hired for the occasion, appeared. She smiled. A swivel chair emerged from nowhere and manoeuvred itself by magic to within an inch of her rump. The lady smiled again and eased herself into it. Then a table swung out in front of her. Very neat. Impressive. She smiled yet again and introduced the sales director of the company who was seated in a chair which also came from the darkness and planted itself at the table. Then the area manager and the production director were likewise slid in to complete the group. All this – the reception, the sets, the technical effects – was accomplished with dazzling professionalism. The cost? Half a million, perhaps more. So far it was worth it. But what followed? What was the core of the show?

What we should have received from the speakers was an exhilarating message powerful enough to inspire us to do business with the company. What we got was an hour of three amateur actors reading excruciatingly badly from three teleprompters and the lady doing her best to inject some point into the proceedings. She failed. Television at its worst consists of talking heads talking drivel. Every time a camera focused on one of these speakers (remember we were watching fifty television screens) he was not with us but searching, eyes down, for his next line. People were kind enough not to laugh outright. It might have been even more embarrassing had the speakers ever made contact with the audience. All that marvellous scenery – the music, the film clips, the skill and the expense – for this rubbish? It was as if a magnificent opera production had been mounted at Covent Garden and the producers had dragged in people off the street to sing the leading parts.

When I enquired what training and rehearsal the speakers in this debacle had received I was told that they had rehearsed 'for a couple of hours on Saturday and a half-day Sunday'. Big deal! A professional communicator would demand more than that.

Companies often call in outside help to act as the anchor-man at their shows. He would normally be a big name perhaps in television or some other part of show business, a fully qualified professional and thoroughly experienced as a communicator – somebody like Frank Bough, who does this sort of thing better than anyone else I know. Mr Bough also has the backing of his own production organization and could, if required, take the whole weight of the event off the shoulders of the presenting company. Star names are expensive, of course, but worth every penny of their fees. They solve many problems for the organizer on the great day and make the occasion bigger, better and truly memorable for the audience.

But what about the other 364 days in the year? Should we tolerate amateurs for all the other occasions? Should the company's own key people be less than professional as communicators?

'Oh, but that means they've got to have time off for training and experience off the job.'

In many companies, manpower has been pared to the bone and company policy insists that nobody can be spared for training and development. 'Every man and woman is indispensable' they bleat. Somebody should tell them that the graveyards are full of indispensable people. How on earth can managers step upwards if they are irreplaceable, immovable and their juniors are kept down, never to rise? At any age and in every job, from top to bottom, people can be groomed to get more business and keep the red blood flowing. Negative attitudes to their greatest asset, their people, is rife in some UK companies. And it shows up in almost everything they do – not only in their presentations. Thank goodness there are enough exceptions to keep our heads above water – but who wants just to tread water?

Lest we grow too sad let us look at success, British success, linked with expert presentations and drive from the top – the Jaguar turnaround.

In 1980: the Jaguar car company was part of British Leyland and suffering a £2–3m loss each month. Productivity was poor: 10,500 employees built 13,800 cars.

Quality and reliability levels were also nothing to be proud of.
The workers' morale was low.

Since the dynamic Sir John Egan took over as the Chairman and Chief Executive that sinking feeling has disappeared. Jaguar is now an independent company.

In 1986: £120m profit in the previous year.
Much improved productivity: 11,000 employees built 43,000 cars.
Reputation for quality and reliability regained and enhanced.
A new product range.
High morale.
Queen's Award for Exports third year running.

The turnaround has been attributed to the following:

Improved manning levels and people working harder (bonus schemes pay well).
Rigorous attention to and resolution of quality problems including more involvement from the shop floor (e.g. Quality Circles).
Improved product design and manufacturing processes.
More training and development.
Better employee communications.
Employee share schemes (they all own a stake in the company).
Higher investment in the company through improved profitability (planned capital spend £100m per annum over the next five years).

Even more to the point, Mr Michael Kinski, Jaguar's Manager, Human Resources, confirms Sir John Egan's broadcast statement that the company now invests more than eight times – that's right, eight times more than the industry norm in developing people.

The brilliantly successful launch of their new car, XJ40, in October 1986 was made possible because Jaguar people are well-trained people. And the company appreciates their worth.

All successful companies present themselves well; presentation is an important factor in their success. Marks and Spencer, ICI, British Petroleum, and others provide splendid models, but I thought it would be simpler to follow through with a single example so that the basic principles of effective presentations emerge more clearly.

The name JCB immediately brings to the mind earth-moving equipment such as backhoe loaders, diggers, crawlers, excavators and other machinery used in the construction and materials handling industries. JCB has become a generic term and the yellow and black livery is seen as a matter of course wherever men dig and build in a big way. Before the initials became public property they belonged to Joseph Cyril Bamford. In a rented lock-up garage, Joe Bamford built with his own hands the first JCB farm trailer. That was in 1945. Today, his company employs a work force of 1700 people manufacturing over 7500 machines a year, using the most advanced production facilities of their kind in Europe.

Perhaps I had better make it clear at this juncture that I have no shares and no hidden interest in praising this company, which is still privately owned and entirely self-financing. But being downright in my comments about what is not good, I must be equally candid – and delighted – about what is good.

It has been said that 'where there's muck there's money'. If you visit the JCB factory in the heart of rural Staffordshire the first thing that strikes you is the complete absence of muck. Can this be a factory – this clinically tidy lakeside building set in 175 acres of fully landscaped countryside?

The second impression is that everybody seems to enjoy working there. Having experienced many first class JCB presentations, I went armed with a list of questions to find out how they tackle the job.

Question 1: When do you decide to invite people to a presentation? What starts the ball rolling?

Answer: As soon as we are sure that we have some additional benefit to offer our customers. What they want is paramount.

Principle 1: The customers and their needs must be prominent in your thinking – from the start.

Question 2: So you don't just get a command from on high to bang the drum?

Answer: No, that would not happen. Anthony has got more sense than that. He would call us together and we'd discuss things first. (Anthony Bamford, son of Joe, is now the managing director of JCB, and held in great esteem even when he's not within earshot. The only type of crawler you do not see in these parts is the human one.)

Principle 2: Presentation is a team job. Involve all who might be concerned as early as possible.

Question 3: What is the usual agenda for your first meeting?

Answer: It varies of course but, roughly speaking, as follows:

(a) Decide the main intention to create a presentation.
(b) What will the customer get out of it?
(c) Who should be invited?
(d) Where? At Rocester (headquarters)? Local road shows for distributors? Abroad, and which countries? Examine all options for locations.
(e) Full current information examined. Get objectives clearly formulated, agreed and written down. By all concerned.

(f) Who does what – various heads delegated to start work and report facts at the next meeting – for progressive action on the structure.

Principle 3: Formulate, discuss and agree on clear common objective. Record it. Check facts. Delegate specific responsibilities. Start action.

Question 4: So you've had a broad brush first meeting. The second meeting brought all the relevant facts – checked – and you've worked out the main structure for the presentation. You have clearly defined your objectives. The various portions of the script have been outlined. What next?

Answer: A script conference to fashion the presentation into a logical to-the-purpose shape. We use the Devil's Advocate method here to ensure that every item is a strength. The time to weed out the weakness is now. Later, it becomes more difficult to cut people out and to correct mistakes.

Principle 4: Be ruthless in eliminating weaknesses. Cut early on.

Question 5: What happens at your structure meeting?

Answer: We hear all the facts, cross fertilize on everyone's ideas and work out the main framework. The full script is designed and heads take responsibility for their own part of the script. Speakers are chosen.

Principle 5: Let everyone know what the others are doing and where his section slots in.

Question 6: Do you at this stage call in an outside producer or outside speakers?

Answer: There is no need. Top management has seen to it that all our key men and women have been equipped as speakers. It's a normal part of our management development programme.

Principle 6: Do not expect speakers to learn only by mistakes made at presentations. Give them

experience beforehand.

Question 7: Does each speaker have an understudy?

Answer: No.

This is a minus point for JCB. Understudies have many values:

(a) The principal speaker might step under a bus or be otherwise rendered out of action.

(b) An understudy is good for the principal. When the understudy is put up during some rehearsals, the principal can see, hear, and be more objective about his part – from the audience's point of view.

(c) It keeps the principal on his toes in direct ratio to the quality of the understudy.

(d) Rehearsals do not become chaotic because one of the principals is unavoidably absent.

(e) It is good development training for the junior.

(f) He can be a useful accessory in checking props and doing other odd jobs for his principal.

Principle 7: Be prepared for emergencies. Never neglect a training opportunity.

Question 8: What about literature – the invitations, the handouts, brochures etc.?

Answer: That is already being taken care of by the department concerned, particularly if we have to go outside for, for instance, specialized printing or other matters beyond our scope.

Talking of outside sources, what do you do about slides, films, TV hook-ups or other special effects?

Answer: We have our own film and TV unit but, if we want something special, we involve outside experts early and tie in their thinking with ours.

Principle 8: Recognize your limitations. Call in help if necessary. Yours is not the only production that outside specialists are working on. If they are any good they are also in demand. So give them time. Get in first. Anticipate delays from any outside source.

Question 9: How do you manage rehearsals?

Answer: Each head makes certain that his section is a strength. He is responsible for seeing that his mechanics, engineers, operators of the machines and all others concerned with the stage management and the equipment know their stuff and that the speakers are well up to the mark. Then we have a day on a piece-at-a-time run through. The stopwatch is well to the fore.

The final or dress rehearsal? We do not subscribe to the old theatrical adage that a bad dress rehearsal means a good show. We keep at it until it's all running smoothly.

Principle 9: Rehearse, rehearse, rehearse, especially props and equipment.

Question 10: Does the audience, subsequent to the show, become involved in demonstrations on site? Do their operators get a chance to work the machines in practical conditions? Is the aftermath – getting the business – well under control?

Answer: Yes. Yes. Yes. Our customers are never left out of anything. It's their show.

Principle 10: Hotelier, Monsieur Ritz, made a fortune from the principle that 'The customer is always right'. 'There's no business like show business.' Without customers there's no business.

JCB's presentation of a new earth-mover will exemplify these principles in action. This massive combination of metal and power offered additional benefits in that it could be operated more easily and that it could work to delicate tolerances. Delicate? An earth-mover? We are considering a rugged machine weighing over seven tons and developing 75 hp: a machine that can dig a trench, shifting 61 metres × 2 metres of solid earth in an hour at any location in all weathers; and without undue strain on the operator. How does one get this across?

During wide-ranging discussions, some genius suggested that power, grace, precision and control were all attributes of a star ballet dancer. Why not a dance of the earth-movers? Sounds absurd but that's what happened – a dance of the earth-movers. It took weeks of preparation.

The performance. To the accompaniment of the band of the Grenadier Guards, eight elephantine machines entered the arena in line ahead and began a routine which would not shame the Bluebell Girls. The machines, expertly operated, moved gracefully into various formations. Some machines extended their arms which met with fingertip precision forming an arch through which the others glided; they sat on their buckets; they manoeuvred like a corps de ballet; they bowed and they bobbed. The whole thing was a delight. Whether the dance was a minuet or a quadrille or both is immaterial. The audience loved it.

If you have not yet seen the subsequent film recording of this remarkable event, you've missed a treat. The important thing is that not only was this presentation a bit of a lark, but it drove home the point that the customer had much to gain when using such a package of power working to fractions of an inch by fingertip controls. The principles we have outlined came into force.

Does a company get results and business from its presentations and a real interest in customers? Well here is one that does.

In the last six years JCB has seen its turnover rise by over 22 per cent with exports accounting for 65 per cent of their business. According to the *Financial Times*, in 'The Top 100 Exporters' league table of UK companies, JCB is the leader of the non-commodity class with an export turnover of £100,381 per employee on the full payroll.

Writing the script

The first thought we must get completely clear is that we are not preparing brochures, reports or other papers meant for reading. Such literature might well be useful as adjuncts to an oral presentation – take-aways for instance – but written English differs in many important respects from that used by successful speakers.

All effective communication results from interplay between people. The writer has some advantages over the speaker, and vice versa. From the start you must make sure that you use all the advantages you have as a speaker – direct communion, direct response, ability to adapt to the situation, repetition and summaries (in the use of which the writer has to be more sparing), physical emphasis, human contact, mobile visual aids, and freer language.

It is not unknown for a sales director to send his underlings out into the world with a rigid script which they must learn by heart and repeat, verbatim, to prospective customers. Oh dear!

In a team job we cannot be free from the necessity to give and to receive cues. Also, the timing of the whole presentation could be ruined by an undisciplined, sloppy speaker wandering lonely as a cloud. Discipline we must have. But no audience likes a succession of robots obviously speaking somebody else's words. This problem must be tackled as soon as the broad outline of the presentation has been agreed. Each speaker should prepare his part to the extent of shaping and arranging his main headings and then speaking, not writing, his contribution. He should try it out with a few colleagues including the stage manager; note and adapt to cues and special effects, time it and rehearse until his part slots in completely with the main line. Then someone can write it. But do not start with a piece of formal writing; it will sound like that. Even Shakespeare worked closely with his actors and wrote to suit the spoken word.

So speak first, get it right for cues, timing etc. Only then commit to paper so that the rest of us know exactly what you are doing and can work with you. This procedure goes for everybody, the bigwigs of the company included.

The audience expects you to know what you are talking about and to feel that your message is for them in particular and not just a yarn for the world at large. This is no occasion for formal proclamation. They want some good news, for themselves, that's all. If you have prepared and rehearsed as suggested you will cut down, if not entirely eliminate, your dependence on scripts, cue cards, teleprompters and other elements that separate you from the agreeable people out front. You will be talking to and for them, personally, and they will appreciate the fact.

As your guests, they will deserve: Invitations in good time, with plentiful information about the location, including the precise address and telephone numbers. How to get there and, if necessary, road maps of the locality, train times and whether you have arranged for them to be met at the station. Parking arrangements. Refreshments. Seat reservations. Starting time. Ending time.

The preliminaries set the atmosphere for your show, especially if your guests are from another country. Mr X, who you will recall let a huge contract get away, lost the battle as early as the preliminaries. The winning competitor had the sense to send, well in advance, a director to visit the customers in their own country. He offered them any location they wished for the presentation. They chose Paris. He also offered the presentation in their choice of language from English, French, Arabic, German or Spanish. They chose English, but they were pleased to have had other options. The director also discussed such matters as diet and places of worship available for the visitors.

Subsequently, the women worshipped in the shops, the lesser orders worshipped at the Folies Bergère and the top brass enjoyed a private show. What chance had Mr X and his lot?

To return to your show. Your customers have arrived, grateful that your directions took the hassle out of the journey and warmed by your welcome. Maybe they've received a cup or a glass of something to lay the dust and you have escorted them to their seats.

Your guests will deserve a reception that confirms their importance. Do not skimp on the number of agreeable helpers available. At the reception the speakers should, if practicable, mix with the guests. This takes the them-and-us edge off the speakers' fear of an audience. They are people, after all, many of them friends; all of them soon will be.

Supporting literature should be available and, if necessary, available in several languages. Do you need simultaneous translation facilities?

Your guests will deserve a production that combines all the elements of successful speaking. Let us sum them up.

1 The whole event has been prepared with your customer in mind. Your own purpose is abundantly clear. That it is achieved is the objective of the exercise.
2 All your people and the equipment have been tried, tested and rehearsed to perfection.
3 The visual aids are clear and memorable.
4 The main facts and the benefits are firmly established so that they are inescapable.

A commercial presentation is a blend of social speaking, specialist talk, talking for business and case presentation – with showbiz trimmings.

You have of course planned the follow-up. Get the business.

10 What now for you?

The patron saint of music, Saint Cecilia, must have wept when Anton Golding lost the use of his nether limbs in a car crash. Here was a man, born to be one of the few among supreme concert pianists, paralysed and useless. The driver of the truck that struck him in New York was admittedly drunk and the American courts had awarded Mr Golding immense damages. But what compensation is there in money when everything you've worked for since the age of six becomes impossible, and savage anger replaces dreams, even hope? For three years he lay flat on his back, kept going only by highly skilled therapy and the devotion of his wife. Slowly he recovered sufficiently to sit in a wheelchair. His hair had gone, so had his teeth. He was a shrivelled, empty shell and spent most of the day morosely staring at nothing. Nobody, not even Mrs Golding, could share his mind. He was no longer with her or anybody else; no longer with the world.

Only those unacknowledged martyrs who nurse severely handicapped people day and night – every day and every night – 365 days and nights, year after year – can appreciate Mrs Golding's suffering. Real living no longer existed for her either. One afternoon, working in the kitchen, she heard a violent crash and a hammering coming from the living room. She hurried in to find Mr Golding, half out of his chair, smashing the lock of the piano. He wrenched up the lid and played a few thundering chords. Then he broke down and cried like a baby. As Mrs Golding held him close to comfort him, a glimmer of relief warmed her. Her husband had, in one of his furies, ordered the piano to be locked and covered out of sight. Those chords were the first he had played for nearly six years.

Mr Golding nodded towards the piano.

'Needs tuning', he grunted.

Hardly daring to speak for fear of provoking an outburst, which had become the norm whenever the piano was mentioned, she replied.

'I'll get Mr Abbott in to do it.'

Mr Abbott duly arrived accompanied by another man. Friends of the stricken pianist always visited in pairs to ensure some sort of dialogue when Golding just stared into space; it was like talking to a vegetable. But this day he conversed normally and agreed that the furniture screening the piano should be removed. The piano lid remained open. Not a note was played on it for three weeks. Mrs Golding made no comment.

She had a new wheelchair built which could be manoeuvred into place as a piano stool. Golding became quite animated as he experimented with the chair. At last, he began to play a few notes. Daily, his wife heard him struggling. Sometimes he would play for hours, sometimes for just a few minutes but always he ended with both fists bashing the keys in fury.

'How the hell can you play a piano without pedalling' he would scream.

Professional musicians have their oddities like the rest of us, but they make wonderful friends. They rallied round Golding to work out new techniques to offset his handicap and the house lived again with the joys of disciplined sound.

Beethoven's deafness precluded him from hearing

performances of his work, but the music in his mind could be written down and appreciated by others. A composer has this satisfaction. An executant musician, a performer, needs an audience in order to be fulfilled. Golding knew that his limitations made concert halls impossible but he played to small groups at home.

The matron of the local hospital asked if he would play for the patients and staff. After much persuasion, he agreed. The performance was a catastrophe because he would stop in the middle of a passage, curse, then play it again and again until he was pleased with it. Then his stamina ran out. Mrs Golding filled in the silence by attempting to explain the difficulties of the piece.

This is where the speaking comes in.

'There must be no going back to his being a prisoner at home', declared Mrs Golding. If she could talk about the music with her husband supplying the examples, he could pace himself and not become exhausted. On good days he would do more and she would talk less. She was a modest lady. 'Is it possible for me to be taught to speak?' she asked. 'Yes.' 'Could the talks be organized in such a way that I could adapt to a new situation at almost every performance?' 'Yes.'

Mrs Golding is a marvel. She studied and worked until she knew every note of music her husband played. She learned about composers and their ways. Friends helped. She became a first class speaker.

She and her husband live modestly in a small country town. Only a few intimates know their story but, about once a month, the Goldings give enormous pleasure to hundreds of local people. Mr Golding no longer dreams of international fame. He has come to terms with the reality of his situation and is content to settle for what he can do well. He knows his deficiencies but you would have to be a skilled musician yourself to spot them. His new-found techniques make pedalling far less important. With her new-found techniques Mrs Golding has blossomed. A great woman. A great partnership. Effective speaking has its uses.

Less tragic, but also troubled, was a man who strode into my office towing a reluctant lady.

'Now,' he snorted. 'Now, perhaps we can get something done about it!'

He went on to explain that the lady was Gillian, his wife, and that he was in the running for a high-level job which meant that his wife would entertain customers, diplomats and other such worthies, and be expected occasionally to say a few words at functions. 'When asked to do so,' he continued, without pausing for breath, 'she blushes like a beetroot and wriggles about howling "I can't, I can't, I can't, and I won't!" We need some help'. Then he added, as an afterthought, 'You do remember me, don't you?'

Indeed, he was remembered. He worked for a company whose board rightly considered that their greatest asset was the people who worked for them. They invested in their development accordingly. We took part in this man's early training as a communicator. He had done well, had Tom.

The story ends on a happy note. After receiving what Tom called 'the treatment', Gillian shed her constricting shell and grew into an excellent speaker, even outshining Tom at times.

Also, pillow talk was resumed.

One of the best lecturers I know is a scientist in Sweden. His body, racked by a wasting disease, is a twisted ruin; but his mind is brilliantly alive. In order to raise his right arm to write on a blackboard he needs to push it slowly upwards and to support it with his left hand. This is only one of his difficulties. Yet this brave man holds his audiences spell-bound. He uses as many devices as possible to reduce physical effort, particularly easily managed visual aids; but it is the structure of his lectures and the way in which he builds our thoughts to match his own which makes him such a good speaker.

If people like Mrs Golding, the howling Gillian and the crippled Swede can speak well, what is to stop you doing so? Many of you can and do; but do you give enough? There are organizations crying out for speakers – business speakers, social speakers, informative speakers. In business you are or could be someone on whom your colleagues can depend for a first class presentation. You are an ambassador, not only for your company but for yourself. On your special subject you could bring pleasure and inside knowledge to, say, Rotary clubs, Round Tables, the Lions, Masonic Lodges, youth clubs, women's organizations, trades unions, adults seeking education, handicapped people, local societies, even to the inmates of prisons and reform schools. You'd be welcomed everywhere. You could share some of your expertise – open up to others a bit of your world. Why not shape a talk at once and make it known that you are available? An effective speaker leads a busy, fulfilled life. He is popular and admired. You'll get your reward if only in human gratitude. Build on the talents you have, and give.

You will recall two questions which were asked at the beginning of this book:

'Do you talk to yourself?'
and
'What on earth prevents you from rising to your feet, say next Tuesday, and giving a first class talk?'

We'll consider, first, the man who is a well-established speaker. He is wise enough to take a searching look at himself at regular intervals to check a few points. Otherwise he could become routine and merely a fellow with years and years of inexperience. We all have to keep a constant watch on ourselves, revise and freshen-up. A Rolls-Royce needs skilled maintenance and even diamonds need cleaning from time to time. No good speaker is ever completely satisfied. There must be no risk that he should ever talk to himself.

But what about those of you who cry 'I can't, I can't. I'm nervous, shy. I've nothing to talk about'? How can you develop confidence and become an effective speaker? First, you can take courage from the examples of Mrs Golding, the howling Gillian and the crippled lecturer. They rose above defeatism and so can you. You probably realize by now that the chief handicap is your focus on yourself and that you must take a positive interest in others.

I know a golfer who always gave his opponents the first hole because he was 'scared of teeing-off in front of all those critics laughing at him from the clubhouse window'. The conceit of it! As if people had nothing better to do but watch his antics. One day, we took him inside the club to examine his fears. The members were playing cards, sleeping, discussing their own prowess and doing nothing at all to indicate an interest in such as he. Our friend cured himself in twenty minutes by driving from the first tee about a hundred balls, then going inside to ask what they thought of his performance. Their replies, such as 'Sorry, old man, I wasn't watching' deflated his ego but demolished his fears for ever.

How many people do you know who can't dance because in their youth they were afraid, literally, to take their first steps in case they were ridiculed? Everyone has to learn. Nobody minds our being novices so long as we have no false pride and at least we are having a go. Everything we do has had to be done for the first time, even breathing. All the world loves a trier, but a girl or boy wriggling about wailing 'I can't and I won't' never learns to dance. Being a wallflower is a self-inflicted wound. So are most undeveloped talents.

I sometimes think when it rains that it is the Good Lord sitting on a damp cloud crying in despair: 'I give people all these talents and they don't bother to develop them.' Just think. You could ease the sufferings of the Almighty. That thought is not so whimsical as it might seem to be. Think about it.

If you are a beginner as a speaker, you would be ill-advised to start with a big occasion. First steps are first steps and must be taken with some care. A sensible skier goes to the pro for lessons and then practises and practises. A learner-driver doesn't leap into a car and speed away; he learns the basics in quiet byways and gains some experience before taking to the highways.

So how can you make a start and build your confidence. One way is to attend as many meetings as you can – in-company meetings, political meetings, social meetings. Watch and listen to the speakers, the chairmen, the members who ask questions. Do they achieve results? If yes, note why and how they do so. When you are ready, take the plunge and ask a question at a meeting. Do not present your question as an attack on the speaker. You should not try to score debating points. Ask for information, guidance. Keep in mind that good speakers welcome pertinent questions. It helps them to clarify matters. Stay on this level as an interested questioner for a few meetings. Get used to the sound of your own voice in public. As soon as you can, graduate to the platform if only as a helper, or perhaps, subsequently to introduce the speaker or to propose a vote of thanks.

Become accustomed to the speaker's view of a meeting. Don't rush things. Attend as many different kinds of meetings as possible – as a questioner, a platform body and as a small-part speaker. If a job arises – for instance, that someone is needed to investigate and report on an item – volunteer at once. At the next meeting you will be making an oral report – speaking in public. You are giving a service as do all effective speakers. Let this element of service colour all your thinking as a speaker.

If you work for a large organization you have many

opportunities to learn and to practise. Join one or more committees; such experience is all grist to the mill. Next, ask your Training Manager to nominate you for a speaking course, run either internally or by outside professionals. Training Managers warm to such requests. They like giving service, too. Should you not have the backing of a company, enquire whether there is a Speakers Club or Toastmasters Club in your district. These amateur clubs can be both instructive and enjoyable. They meet in a local tea room or a pub. The members present brief talks and make constructive comments on each other's performances. After a few evenings with the Toastmasters (not to be confused with the dignified gentlemen working at banquets) or the Speakers Club, you will have found your feet and perhaps be surprised that you had so much talent.

You should now be ready to consider the real thing, a talk in public.

'But what can I talk about?' you ask. That's a fair question. What do you know?

A young lady who works as a small cog in a unit producing wildlife features for television became bored between jobs. Life for her was blank unless she was busy in some remote part of the world recording the marvels we look at on the box almost every day. Instead of twiddling her thumbs she devised a talk about the inner workings of a television production and is now in demand as a speaker. Life is no longer bleak. She is immensely popular and has no time to be bored between assignments. Of course, she has the advantage of wonderful pictures and she can name famous names. But the point is that she is using, not neglecting, such advantages.

Here are some more examples of people who broadened their own horizons by bringing interest and knowledge to others.

A medical man who talks about fishing at youth clubs.

A woman who teaches others about cake making. (Her

impact at ending is our enjoying of the product – mouth-watering stuff.)

A broker revealing inside information about the workings of the Stock Exchange.

A young woman who takes us deep into the caves and potholes of Derbyshire.

A shop assistant who talks about make-up.

The opportunities and the subjects are limitless. No aspect of life is without interest. There are about 30,000 organizations in Great Britain needing speakers – speakers explaining professional matters, social speakers, informative speakers; speakers who can take us to the inside of police work, ambulance work and first aid; the inner workings of a top football club, flower arrangement, talks about the famous and the infamous; guided tours, local and national history; a stage manager talking to drama groups. Subjects such as travel and adventure, photography, handicrafts, sports, mountaineering, sailing, politics – both local and international; formation dancing; life for an Australian girl in London; life for a Londoner in Peckham; religious matters, ethnic matters; upholstery, embroidery, knitting, carpentry, bricklaying, wine making, animal care and training . . . .

There are at least ten good talks in everyone. Choose a subject that you know about or can research. Do something this very day. This could be the first day of your life as a speaker. Shape a talk and offer your services. Bring knowledge, joy and a glimpse into the new for the many. Be yourself, your true self, the whole person, not just a half.

Don't worry about speaking. Work at it. Re-read this book and have a go.

Some thoughts

Make contact with people. Use your eyes. Look at them. Include them in what you say. This is simply good manners. Take the trouble to prepare properly to ensure that you give them value in exchange for the time they are giving you. Develop a respect, even an affection for your audience. Remember that, however expert you may be, every man and woman there is superior to you in some way and could teach you something. Equally, people like to be on the receiving end of someone else's knowledge.

There are few things more exhilarating than an audience reacting with interest, excitement and the sheer pleasure of enjoying a first class speaker. Deserve such a reaction and your world will be that much better for having you around.

I offer you a final handshake. Good luck.

Index